Elements and Dimensions of an Ericksonian Approach

Ericksonian Monographs

Elements and Dimensions of an Ericksonian Approach

Edited by Stephen R. Lankton

Brunner/Mazel Publishers • New York

Library of Congress Cataloging-in-Publication Data
Main entry under title:

Elements and dimensions of an Ericksonian approach.

  (Ericksonian Monographs; monograph no. 1)
  Includes bibliographies.
  1. Hypnotism — Therapeutic use.   2. Psychotherapy.
3. Erickson, Milton H.   I. Lankton, Stephen R.
II. Series.
RC495.E38 1985   616.89′162   85-17454
ISBN 0-87630-411-0

Published by
BRUNNER/MAZEL, INC.
19 Union Square
New York, New York 10003

MANUFACTURED IN THE UNITED STATES OF AMERICA

Ericksonian Monographs

Ericksonian Monographs publishes only original manuscripts dealing with Ericksonian approaches to hypnosis, family therapy, and psychotherapy, including techniques, case studies, research and theory.

The *Monographs* will publish only those articles of highest quality that foster the growth and development of the Ericksonian approach and exemplify an original contribution to the fields of physical and mental health. In keeping with the purpose of the *Monographs*, articles should be prepared so that they are readable to a heterogeneous audience of professionals in psychology, medicine, social work, dentistry and related clinical fields.

Publication of the *Ericksonian Monographs* shall be on an irregular basis; no more than three times per year. The *Monographs* are a numbered, periodical publication. Dates of publication are determined by the quantity of high quality articles accepted by the Editorial Board and the Board of Directors of the Milton H. Erickson Foundation, Inc., rather than calendar dates.

Manuscripts should be *submitted in quintuplicate* (5 copies) with a 100–150-word abstract to Stephen R. Lankton, M.S.W., P.O. Box 958, Gulf Breeze, Florida 32561-0958. Manuscripts of length ranging from 15 to 100 typed double-spaced pages will be considered for publication. Submitted manuscripts cannot be returned to authors. Authors with telecommunication capability may presubmit one copy electronically in ASCII format at either 1200 or 300 baud rate and the following communication parameters: 8 bit word size, No parity, 1 stop bit, x-on/x-off enabled, ascii and xmodem transfer protocols are acceptable. Call (904) 932-6819 to arrange transmission and obtain the necessary security password.

Style and format of submitted manuscripts must adhere to instructions described in the *Publication Manual of the American Psychological Association* (3rd edition, 1983). The manuscripts will be returned for revision if reference citations, preparation of tables and figures, manuscript format, avoidance of sexist language, copyright permission for cited material, title page style, etc. do not conform to the *Manual*.

Copyright ownership must be transferred to the Milton H. Erickson Foundation, Inc., if your manuscript is accepted for publication. The Editor's acceptance letter will include a form explaining copyright release, ownership and privileges.

Reference citations should be scrutinized with special care to credit originality and avoid plagiarism. Referenced material should be carefully checked by the author prior to first submission of the manuscript.

Charts and photographs accompanying the manuscripts must be presented in camera-ready form.

Copy editing and galley proofs will be sent to the authors for revisions. Manuscripts must be submitted in clearly written, acceptable, scholarly English. Neither the Editor nor the Publisher is responsible for correcting error of spelling and grammar: the manuscript, after acceptance, should be immediately ready for publication. Authors should understand there will be a charge passed on to them by the Publisher for revision of galleys.

Prescreening and review procedures for articles is outlined below. Priority is given to those articles which conform to the designated theme for the upcoming *Monographs*. All manuscripts will be prescreened, absented of the author's name, by the Editor or one member of the Editorial Board and one member of either the Continuing Medical Education Committee or the Board of Directors of the Milton H. Erickson Foundation, Inc.

Final acceptance of all articles is done at the discretion of the Board of Directors of the Milton H. Erickson Foundation, Inc. Their decisions will be made after acceptable prescreened articles have been reviewed and edited by a minimum of four persons: two Editorial Board members, one member of the CME Committee or the Board of Directors, and the Editor. Occasionally, reviewers selected by the Editor will assist in compiling feedback to authors.

Feedback for authors and manuscript revision will be handled by the Editor usually between one and two months after submission of the prepared manuscript. Additional inquiries are welcomed if addressed to the Editor.

Contents

Contributors

William O. Bank, M.D.
Director of Medical Imaging, Computerized Medical Imaging Center, Sherman Oaks, CA

D. Corydon Hammond, Ph.D.
Co-director, Sex and Marital Therapy Clinic, and Assistant Professor, Physical Medicine and Rehabilitation, University of Utah School of Medicine, Salt Lake City, UT

Carol H. Lankton, M.A.
Private practice and training; Faculty, Department of Psychology, University of West Florida, Pensacola, FL

Stephen R. Lankton, M.S.W.
Private practice and training; Faculty, Department of Psychology, University of West Florida, Pensacola, FL

William J. Matthews, Ph.D.
Assistant Professor, Counseling Psychology, University of Massachusetts, Amherst, MA

Ernest L. Rossi, Ph.D.
Private practice; Training Analyst, C. G. Jung Institute, Los Angeles, CA

Michael D. Yapko, Ph.D.
Director, Milton H. Erickson Institute, San Diego, CA

Jeffrey K. Zeig, Ph.D.
Director, Milton H. Erickson Foundation, Phoenix, AZ

Foreword

As this first issue of the *Ericksonian Monographs* is published, I know that, were Milton H. Erickson still alive, he would be extremely proud of this achievement. My father enjoyed progress and accomplishments and the rewards of work and effort. The *Monographs* will serve as a portion of the educational forum of the Milton H. Erickson Foundation, an expansion of the Foundation's efforts to render information to professionals in a readily accessible manner. This publication will provide an opportunity for the exchange of ideas, knowledge and experiences relating to the field of Ericksonian hypnosis and family therapy. Finally, my father would have appreciated any effort that furthered the ethical use of his approach.

It is the hope of our Foundation that this publication will always reflect the fundamental principles that we understand and identify as Milton H. Erickson's philosophy. *The most important aspect of this philosophy is the concept of the individuality of the therapist and the individuality of the patient.* My father encouraged others not to mimic him, but rather to incorporate into one's knowledge the skills and techniques that reflected one's personal abilities and interests. My father envisioned the therapist's role as a guide since the patient has within him the correct solution for his particular self and situation. Therefore, as guides constantly faced with new journeys and predicaments, therapists must be at all times practical, observant, and resourceful.

My father and mother loved information and knowledge of all kinds. They strongly fostered the notion in their children that it is exciting and fun to learn.

It is our hope that those many, many persons who share our interest in Ericksonian theory and techniques will not only find this Monograph Series informative and educational, but also enjoy it as an exciting way of learning.

Kristina K. Erickson, M.D.
Vice-President, Board of Directors
Milton H. Erickson Foundation, Inc.

April, 1985
Columbia, MO

Editor's Preface to Monograph No. 1

Elements and Dimensions of an Ericksonian Approach

The mandate for the *Ericksonian Monographs* is to expand and promote the work and influence created by Dr. Erickson. Yet his work is not easily understood; ironically, this may be because he was solution-oriented and practical. Erickson's decidedly unique approach is unprecedented in the history of therapy. For some, Erickson's work can be difficult to grasp because it operates from heuristic, problem-solving procedures. For many, this approach may represent a different philosophical stance toward therapy and change. Many practitioners rely upon a cause and effect model of intervention or approach therapy only in terms of reified constructs of personality. For those individuals, Erickson's work will appear to be, as Haley put it, an uncommon therapy.

Erickson disapproved of *schools of therapy*. As much as possible he avoided jargon that was taken from any particular school. He believed that a school presents *the* right ways to do therapy. In each school the *other* ways of doing things are wrong; many effective techniques are avoided or misunderstood. Each school defends its procedures, premises, dictates, theory, and research in order to establish a sort of territory of expertise and, possibly, to promote financial survival of its members.

Clients all too often pay a price for the profession's territorialism. This price is the loss of individuality, talent, and experience when clients are forced to fit into what Erickson (1979) referred to as the Procrustean bed. "Each person is a unique individual. Hence, psychotherapy should be formulated to meet the uniqueness of the individual's needs, rather than tailoring the person to fit the Procrustean bed of a hypothetical theory of human behavior." He enjoyed demonstrating how various psychological theories are limited by their own preconceived constructs. He wanted to tailor the bed to fit the person and repeatedly stated that he created a new theory for each client.

That same spirit of intellectual freedom is demonstrated in the work of the authors appearing in this issue. We intend that it become the hallmark of the *Ericksonian Monographs*.

All of the articles in *Monograph No. 1* are original and deal with the theme *Elements and Dimensions of an Ericksonian Approach*. Some authors have given examples from Erickson's own work and others have provided interpretations of their own. Yet, a comparison of these articles reveals agreement on some fundamental concepts of a distinctive approach. These concepts define and identify the work of Erickson as well as the work of those authors who have incorporated his influence throughout their work. In the final analysis, this is the Ericksonian approach as it is understood today.

The foundation of an Ericksonian approach, according to these authors, rests on several pillars that include: utilization of client behaviors; indirection techniques, including suggestions and stories; strategic therapy; a naturalistic approach; reliance upon anecdotes to promote personal understanding; utilization of the reality context, and a reliance upon the values of action, effort, and enjoyment. The authors come from many perspectives and approaches to treatment including medicine, psychology, social work, family therapy, hypnotherapy and psychiatry.

It is not surprising that the Ericksonian approaches presented in this volume deal with more than hypnotherapy. There is documentation for medical applications by William Bank who has provided a photo X-ray demonstration for the control of bleeding using Ericksonian suggestions. Carol Lankton has presented a thoughtful examination of the principles of Erickson's approach from the therapist's viewpoint. One of Erickson's previously unpublished educational and training examples is elucidated by Ernest Rossi. A theoretical model of states of consciousness in individual and family therapy is contributed by Stephen Lankton and will help link hypnotherapy and family therapy. Jeffrey Zeig presents several anecdotes relating personal views of the impact that Erickson made on students, trainees and clients. William Matthews examines Erickson's work from a cybernetic model that illustrates many tactics setting Erickson's work apart and explaining the role therapists play in affecting the reality they perceive with their clients. Michael Yapko presents an overview of hypnotic and nonhypnotic interventions aimed at helping depressed individuals. An application of Erickson's perspective, adapted to a unique diagnostic aid, is presented by Corydon Hammond. Finally, Milton Erickson himself is represented by a previously unpublished article on certain principles of medical hypnosis, contributed by Mrs. Elizabeth Erickson.

It is a rare pleasure to present the first issue of this new publication. We anticipate that the *Ericksonian Monographs* will make a contribution in the multidisciplinary fields of mental health. My excitement has grown throughout the many phases of developing this first issue. It began with organizing the staff of Editorial Board Members comprised of distinguished and creative professionals, many of whom are internationally renowned.

Manuscripts were then invited and received in the months that followed. The manuscripts represented the current work of theorists, family therapists, hypnotherapists, anthropologists, and physicians who are in the forefront of what may well be the most rapidly growing influence in the field of therapy. thropologists, and physicians who are on the forefront of what may well be the most rapidly growing influence in the field of therapy.

It was most rewarding to observe that Dr. Erickson's legacy is appreciating through applications of his approaches by thousands of therapists worldwide. These practitioners represent implementations of his ideas in many realms of therapy. The work in this issue is a partial representation of the state of the art of therapy in the 1980s and I cannot help but wonder what understandings the future will hold when our language and perception advances. Perhaps we will become even more able to profit from Erickson's creative genius and the integration of his work into family and individual therapy. I look forward to the future of the *Ericksonian Monographs* as a vehicle that will contribute to the comprehension and practice of effective therapy.

Gulf Breeze, Florida   Stephen R. Lankton
April, 1985

Reference

ERICKSON, M. H. (1979). First International Congress (conference brochure). Phoenix: Milton H. Erickson Foundation, Inc.

Memory and Hallucination (Part 1): The Utilization Approach to Hypnotic Suggestion

Milton H. Erickson, M.D.

with Introduction, Commentaries, and Discussion by
Ernest L. Rossi, Ph.D.

This paper provides an example of how Erickson utilized resistance and a sub-ject's own memories and associative processes to facilitate positive and neg-ative hallucinatory experience. The role of social context and personal associ-ations in memory and hallucination is illustrated. Suggestions are made about the process of learning to *utilize* rather than merely *analyze* a subject's inter-nal mental mechanisms and memories to facilitate hypnotic phenomena.

This fascinating though incomplete fragment about the process of evoking hallucinations was included in a box of incomplete manuscripts which Erick-son entrusted to me during the period in which his *Collected Papers* (Rossi, 1980) were being edited (the late 1970s). I was able to edit most of those in-complete manuscripts into publication form for the *Collected Papers*. How-ever, a few of them, such as the fragment that is the basis of this paper, were not really understood at the time and so were not included. I recently discov-ered that I had audio recorded a discussion of this fragment with two other professional visitors back in 1976. This discussion forms the body of the com-mentaries that I have now added to the original fragment to create this paper.

Address reprint requests to: Ernest L. Rossi, Ph.D., 23708 Harbor Vista, Malibu, CA 90265.

The significance of this paper derives from the emphasis it places on three aspects of Erickson's utilization approach to hypnotic suggestion:

1) The hypnotic state is an experience that belongs to the subject.
2) Deep trance experience involves a utilization of the subject's memories of well-motivated life experience ("experiential learnings").
3) Mental mechanisms are evoked and utilized to facilitate the acceptance of hypnotic suggestion.

We will return to these three basic elements in the Discussion section of this paper, after we have seen how Erickson actually uses them to facilitate profound somnambulistic trance and hallucinatory behavior in his subject.

In what follows I am adopting the same conventions of presentation that Erickson and I developed in our books. The titles to each section are mine. The text under each title is from Erickson's unfinished paper, just as he originally wrote it. The only editorial liberty I took in this regard was to divide Erickson's original and unedited material into sections corresponding to our commentaries on it and to italicize those words, phrases, or sentences which were pertinent to the commentaries.

It appears from the contents of this paper that Erickson wrote it during the 1960s when he published his major paper on hypnotic and nonhypnotic realities (Erickson, 1967). While editing this material for publication, I added further summarizing commentaries in 1984. All commentaries are highly edited for readability. Irrelevant portions of our conversations were eliminated. Erickson's words are verbatim (though on occasion slightly rearranged), but the words of the other participants are sometimes shortened and/or clarified.

Accepting, Actualizing, and Depotentiating Resistance and the Negative as a Precondition for Facilitating Hypnotic Experience

Erickson's paper begins as follows:

E: Another incident pertinent to the subject of *hypnotic and nonhypnotic realities* concerns a college sophomore student who hesitantly volunteered as a subject by stating, *"I am very sure you cannot hypnotize me."* Since *this was an expression of a negative attitude, it was properly respected by the simple process of asking her to look at the rear wall of the classroom and to visualize mountain scenery, pine trees, snow, and rocks.*

She apologetically stated that no matter how hard she tried, she just couldn't do it. *The tone of her voice and her general bearing indicated that she would like to do something positively, since the author had allowed her to do a negative thing very well.*

Rossi (R): [1984] Since the subject begins with doubt and a negative set, Erickson apparently begins by giving her a visualization task at which she can fail. This failure "satisfies" her negative set so that she is then ready to do something positive.

Visitor (V): We don't have the actual words to demonstrate the way Erickson said that in the manuscript. Could you give an example of what you might say to permit a failure?

Erickson (E): S was a student who wanted to learn a lot about different hypnotic phenomena. She wanted to learn *all* the hypnotic phenomena. [To permit failure I might say,] "And one subject necessarily *can't* demonstrate *all* hypnotic phenomena . . . I'll *try* to offer you . . . *perhaps* by looking at that wall you *may* be able to visualize some scene. You *try* hard."

V: So you've got four blocks in there: *try, perhaps, may*, and the introductory remark that *you can't learn them all*.

E: When I first asked S to be my subject she said she couldn't be. She was on the debate team and she was keenly interested in everything. [So I said to her,] "Have you any idea of how interested you are in hypnosis? And you're going to be interested in plenty of it."

R: So you utilized and generalized her attitude of "I'm interested in everything" to include hypnosis.

E: She came up and said, "I don't really believe I can." I said, "Well, I believe you can." How can you dispute that statement? There's no way you can dispute it!

R: Except that she could say that you are a fool for believing such a thing and thus negate you.

E: Yes, but still, *I believe* — you *can't* negate that. She can call me a fool but regardless, *I* do believe. There is no way of getting around that, and it's a very *disconcerting* thing.

R: So you were shaking up her mental sets; that was a way of coping with the doubts of her conscious mind. You were depotentiating her doubts.

R: [1984 Summary] She volunteers as a hypnotic subject and presumably wants to have a positive experience. She demonstrates that she is not able to deal with her own negative mental set, however, when she says, "I am very sure you cannot hypnotize me." Erickson does not respond to this as if it were a resistance challenging his authority, competence, or prestige. Instead he accepts it for what it is: the confession of a learned limitation by the subject whose belief system and life experience do not permit her to experience the reality of hypnosis yet. Erickson does not try to deny the reality or power of this negative mental set. Instead he fully accepts its validity and proceeds to facilitate a self-fulfilling expression of it: He asks her to visualize mountain scenery on the rear of the classroom and permits her negative mental set its full expression by allowing her to fail.

This is an example of one of Erickson's most original contributions to the practice of psychotherapy: He does not analyze or discuss the subject's negative mental set as a "faulty attitude" or a "resistance." Instead, he arranges circumstances that permit the negative set to discharge itself fully so that another mental set (in this case a positive wish for hypnotic experience) can come into focal consciousness and be actualized into behavior. Erickson immediately proceeds to give her an opportunity to actualize this positive wish with his suggestions in the next section.

Erickson may have developed this approach from his early experimental studies on word association, induced complexes, and experimental neuroses using the Luria Technique (Erickson, 1935, 1936, 1944; Huston, Shakow, & Erickson, 1934). There seems to be the same general law of associative psychology governing all these different levels of mental process: Only after a momentarily dominant word association, mental set, or frame of reference has been fully expressed can another process on that level come into focal consciousness and be actualized into behavior.

Utilizing the Present Tense to Induce a Hallucinatory Experience: Negative Implication Leading to a Failure of "Suggestion" in the Somnambulistic State: Many Levels of Awareness in Deep Hypnotic Experience

E: The statement was made to her, "I do not know where you live, but you are attending college and since you are a sophomore, you have reached that age in which you have undoubtedly found some restaurant at which you like to dine, perhaps some restaurant that serves a food that you enjoy very much." Her reply was, "Yes, there is a restaurant in Glendale where they serve chicken and that chicken is really very good." I stated, "Yes it is, isn't it?" Unhesitatingly she said, "As usual, I enjoy eating here," and the class was surprised by her apparent chewing. *They did not realize the importance of the use of the present tense in inducing a trance.*

The author [Erickson] continued, "Actually this restaurant has more than one attraction, doesn't it?" Toying with her hand she said, "I like the guitarist there. He really plays so well. I do enjoy his music." I asked, "Is he playing now?" She said, "No, it is his rest period. But very shortly he will be back and I can eat this chicken and enjoy knowing that shortly he will return from his rest period. He really plays beautifully. I am sure you will enjoy it too." I then asked her, *"Is it still impossible for you to see the mountains on the back wall of the classroom?"* She said, *"I will try again."* After a considerable effort she said apologetically, "I just can't visualize the mountain scene there, but this chicken is very good and it isn't going to be long before the guitarist gets here."

The author indicated to the class [members] that any one of them might speak to her. One member asked her, "Is the chicken good?" She told him, "It is really very good. Why don't you order some?" Astounded by this reply, he asked her if she was eating chicken and she answered very simply, "Of course, and it is very good." At this point the author interrupted, "I see the guitarist has picked up his guitar," to which she said, "I am glad; I do enjoy the music."

Other members of the class endeavored to break down the situation. The girl knew that she was in a restaurant. She knew that she was eating chicken. She knew that she was listening to the guitarist, and she showed frank bewilderment at the doubts expressed by the class. *When the author again asked her if she could visualize the mountain scene on the back wall of the classroom she said, "I will try again." After straining hard she said, "No matter how hard I try, I just simply can't do it."* To this the author said, *"I think it is much more enjoyable to sit down and to listen to the guitarist,"* to which she stated, *"It certainly is."*

While the class members studied and tried hard to make some sense out of this behavior, they endeavored to get the author to explain. Turning away from the girl so that she was excluded as a listener, the explanation was given:

"Everyone of you can dream. In those dreams you can talk to very real people. You can eat very real steaks. You can enjoy dancing with delightful partners. You can fly a plane. You can go for a swim. You can listen to a concert and during the dream you never once say to yourself, 'Now is that person a real person?' You accept your visual, auditory, and all other sensual experiences as real, and you have a good time."

The author pointed out that *a person can function at various levels of awareness*; that one can see a very dear friend across the room whom he met at the opera and unconsciously tap out with his fingers the beat of the particular piece of music he most enjoyed at the opera, quite unaware of what his fingers are doing. And he can actually become embarrassed when his attention is drawn to his behavior. It was also pointed out that the experiences of life are not just those of physical reality. There are also experiential events in the life of a person; given the proper stimulation, the past experiential values considered forgotten, unavailable, or impossible to discover can be brought forth very easily.

R: [1984] Now that the subject is in a somnambulistic state and actively hallucinating the experience of eating chicken in a restaurant and listening to music, Erickson tried for a second time to evoke the visual hallucination of a mountain scene. One would think that this rich somnambulistic state would be a sufficient condition for her to accept Erickson's suggestion. But notice that he again offers his suggestion with an imbedded negative qualifier when he says, "Is it *still impossible* for you to see the mountain . . . " The subject again responds with the negative mental set, "I will *try* again," and naturally fails again.

A question and answer period follows in which students in the class question her and attempt to break down the somnambulistic state. Her hypnotic reality is so well entrenched, however, that they cannot disturb it. Here Erickson makes a third effort to suggest her visualization of the mountain scene. We do not have his actual words at this point, but it is obvious that the subject fails again. Her negative mental set again expresses itself when she repeats, "I will *try* again . . . No matter how hard I *try*, I just simply can't do it."

Erickson now allows the subject to recover from this possibly disconcerting failure by telling her, "I think it is much more enjoyable to sit down and to listen to the guitarist." It was highly characteristic of Erickson to intersperse these periods of "enjoyment" to reinforce subjects for their effort and to deepen trance when its integrity is threatened by their inability to follow a suggestion. The value of this enjoyment is certainly supported by this subject's empathic agreement, "It certainly is."

Social Context as a Factor in Associative Memory: The Name Association Experiment

R: [1984] While the integrity of the trance is being reestablished by letting the subject hallucinate the enjoyable guitar music, Erickson next gives the class a description of a field experiment demonstrating the importance of social context in associative memory. The lengthy description of this experiment in this section may seem to be an irrelevant disruption of the trance work but, in fact, it is actually an indirect way of suggesting to the subject that she do something analogous with her associations during this period of trance deepening. A more detailed example of how he could offer a series of indirect suggestions under the guise of giving an objective lecture about hypnosis is provided by his Ocean Monarch talk on Hypnosis in Psychiatry (Erickson & Rossi, 1981).

E: To illustrate this point the author stated that he had spent a week writing down all the names of the patients he could recall during the period of time he had worked at a certain hospital. Each day he allowed himself to add a few more names, but the last three days proved to yield no more names. However, the author knew that two associates who had been on the staff of that hospital with him would be visiting on a certain day. Accordingly he instructed his secretary to meet the first arrival, take him to a room by himself, and hand him a pencil and paper, saying, "Dr. Erickson has asked me to tell you to write down the names of all the patients you remember during the period of service at the Worcester State Hospital." She treated the second arrival in the same manner. Both of these associates were accustomed to the author's unexpected experimental studies.

When the first arrival had exhausted his memory of names, the secretary brought him into the author's office with the statement, "Do not speak to Dr. Erickson. He will not speak to you. As further names come to mind, write them down." As the doctor sat down at a second desk he promptly added a considerable number of names to his list, even as the author did. The secretary then took the physician to yet another office and told him to wait for further instructions. Next she brought the second physician into the author's office, giving him the same instructions. He, too, immediately added additional names to his list, as did the author.

When the second visitor found himself at a loss to remember any further names, the secretary said, "Come with me. I will take you to another office. There are to be no spoken words. You will simply write down any further names you remember." She took him to the office where the first visitor was waiting with his list of names, and both at once silently added still further names to the lists. When they had exhausted their memories, the secretary brought them both into the author's office and the three of us silently added still further names to the lists. Neither of the other two physicians had expected to encounter the other. Only the author knew that they were both arriving on the same day.

Finally, when all three of us had silently searched our memories, we then noted the memories we had recovered alone, the memories recovered in association with each of the other separately, and then the additional memories recovered when all three of us were present. We had an unbelievable discovery of all the unexpected and unknown stimuli that could elicit otherwise unattainable memories.

R: [1984] This experiment on the influence of social context in relation to associative memory was published for the first time in the *Collected Papers* as a portion of Erickson's paper, "Notes on Minimal Cues in Vocal Dynamics and Memory" (Erickson, 1980). Erickson's presentation of this material to his class in this context illustrates how strongly he believed that hypnotic "suggestions" for hallucinatory behavior needed to be grounded in the utilization of the subject's real memories, associative processes, and "experiential knowledge." Relying upon the hypnotherapist's personal associations and frames of reference in evoking another's hallucinatory experience simply would not do. This is the basic difference between the *utilization approach* to hypnotic suggestion and the "pure suggestion" approach.

The Appropriate Use of Words
in Creating Situations for Utilizing Memories
to Facilitate Hallucinatory Behavior

E: An analogy of this was drawn in comparison with the subject's behavior. Certainly she had an experiential knowledge of the classroom and of the class. She also had an experiential knowledge of the restaurant, of eating chicken, of listening to music, and of talking to a companion. These were separate and discrete memories. She also had a separate and discrete memory of an effort to visualize a mountain landscape on the rear wall of the classroom. *Not one of these separate and discrete memories was dependent upon any other. They each belonged to a totally separate experience.* She could answer questions put to her by the members of the class while she was seemingly eating chicken because she had a separate, discrete memory of having answered questions put to her by the members of the class in the ordinary waking state. *All that the author did was to create a situation in which he could vivify and elicit past learning and experiences as being currently experienced and [to facilitate] the subject's shift from one set of memories to another by an appropriate use of words.*

At the conclusion of the demonstration the author said, "Now let's return to the classroom." In a rather startled way the young woman said aloud, "What has been going on? My mouth feels as if I have just been eating chicken. I can taste it vividly." A member of the class asked, "Does any type of music come to your mind?" In a rather apologetic voice she said, "It seems as if I have just been listening to a guitarist in a restaurant in Glendale, but I know I have been here all evening. I know I haven't been eating chicken. I know I haven't been listening to a guitarist. All I know is that I simply cannot visualize a mountain landscape on the classroom wall." The question was asked, "Can you be hypnotized?" She replied, "I don't think so, but maybe Dr. Erickson would like to try to put me in a trance."

R: [1984] This section continues to illustrate how Erickson's thinking was firmly based on the classical associational view of memory. Hypnotic experience is facilitated by first evoking the subject's personal memory systems and then by creating situations in which those systems can be acted out, reified, or actualized as a current reality. For Erickson, it is the subject's real-life "experiential learnings," rather than imagination *per se*, that are the raw material of hypnotic experience (Rossi, Ryan, & Sharp, 1983; Erickson & Rossi, 1977).

Truisms Accessing and Activating Associative Memories as a Precondition for Hallucinatory Experience: Displacing Resistance by Allowing Failure First

E: On another occasion when this young woman served as a clerk for the class, she was called up to the front and asked to take a seat beside the author. The question was put to her, "You have your doubts about my inducing a trance in you?" She answered, "I don't want to be rude, but I don't think you can. I don't think anybody can hypnotize me."

In reply the author said: *"On many occasions you have looked into a mirror to see how your dress or your blouse looked. You have had no hesitation whatsoever about looking in the mirror to observe whether or not the colors of the blouse suited the color of the shirt."*

She remarked wonderingly, *"That's true. I know it is true, but I don't know what you are getting at."*

The author answered, *"In looking at yourself in the mirror, studying your blouse and skirt to see if the colors were suitable, you also saw your face, and perhaps if it was a full-length mirror, you even saw your feet. In the process of looking at yourself in a mirror, you developed a visual*

memory of how you looked sitting down studying your mirrored image
to make certain that your appearance was in good taste. "

R: You reinduce the original trance situation by reminding her of her initial
doubts about trance and she again expresses these doubts about your ability to hypnotize her. This time you apparently ignore her negative set
and simply proceed with a series of truisms: "On many occasions you
have looked into a mirror to see how your dress or your blouse looked,"
and so forth. This is a truism and it must evoke real associative memories within her. You continue with a series of remarks that are probably true of any young woman looking into a mirror at herself; all are
truisms. You are developing a *yes* set so that "she remarked wonderingly, 'That's true . . . but I don't know what you are getting at.' "

What you're actually "getting at" is a mobilization and activation of
those visual memories that she will use in a moment or two for the hallucination you are going to suggest.

E: [Nods yes] And in addition, having her fail to visualize the mountains.
When you fail somebody you like, then you [are more likely to do something else they request].

R: Right, so you are also discharging resistance again by allowing her to express her doubt first?

E: Yes, that failure before . . .

R: By allowing her to first express her negative set, you are mobilizing a wish
to succeed next time.

Surprise, Curiosity, Anxiety and Compulsion
to Facilitate Self-Hallucinations;
Multiple Levels of Awareness; A Subtle Test
for the Validity of Visual Hallucinations

E: [The author continues] *"Now I am going to give you a surprise, although*
I think you will be rather hesitant to discover it. But your curiosity will
compel you to do it. Over there in a chair about six feet away from you.
When you develop enough courage, you will see yourself sitting there."
The subject gave an excellent, naive, unsophisticated portrayal of a hesitant but compelling curiosity. She finally succeeded in looking at the chair
and remarked, "I am too sitting over there, but I am really sitting here,
but I see myself sitting over there." She turned to the author and said,
"But that isn't possible." To this the author said, *"Even more astonishing*

will be the fact that you will see yourself standing behind the chair in which you are sitting." Again she manifested a compelling curiosity and said, "I am standing behind myself, or I am sitting in the chair. From where I am standing, I am wearing my black skirt. From where I am sitting, I am wearing my blue skirt. And over here I am wearing my red skirt. There aren't three of us but I see all three of us!"

R: I would like you to give a commentary on your approach to inducing this visual hallucination of the subject sitting in the chair six feet away from where she is actually sitting, and then simultaneously seeing herself standing behind her hallucinated self in the chair. This engages three separate self-images.

E: Alright. What does a girl look at when she looks in a mirror?

R: She looks at herself.

E: In what state of dress? [Pause] Removing her makeup, putting on her nightie, taking off her nightie. All the mirror images that she has seen lead into all other mirror images.

R: I see. Your mention of her experience with looking at her blouse and skirt in the mirror actually pulls in all possible mirror associations. You are activating those visual memory banks before you give the suggestion for a visual hallucination. In that way the memories are in a state of readiness to respond. Right?

E: Yes, and it's going to be a big relief. I don't say what surprising thing it will lead to. It might be her breasts.

R: Now, where in the world are you going with that?

E: You see, every girl looks in the mirror at her breasts.

R: I see. She might now have the private thought, "Oh, my goodness, is he going to talk about my breasts?" Or she might simply blush and not know why because of a vague feeling of embarrassment evoked by the intimacy and privacy associated with your mirror analogy. You arouse a half-conscious, half-unconscious anxiety?

E: A *surprise*, isn't it! A fright!

R: A fright?! You arouse a potentially threatening situation?

E: Yes. I make it a surprise and then I make it sitting in a chair . . .

R: . . . which is a great relief compared to the potential fright.

E: She's going to *want* to do that!

R: She is going to want to see herself sitting in a chair rather than be asked something embarrassing, such as having to see her breasts bare!

E: That's right!

R: You proceed with, " . . . although I think you will be hesitant to discover it . . . " She is hesitant at this point so you are using another truism. "But your curiosity will compel you to do it." You are utilizing her curiosity at the end of this truism.

V: But that doesn't answer the threat.

E: Oh, yes [it does].

V: By telling her that she'll only be hesitant instead of feeling worse things?

E: I saw the way her head began to move.

R: I see. You saw her head moving back and forth anxiously?

E: Here was a shy girl. . . . Then she gave a deep sigh when she saw . . .

R: . . . it was going to be a safe thing to look at herself sitting in a chair?

E: Um-hum.

R: Okay. So you really fixated her attention with anxiety-provoking comments, hesitancy, and surprise. Then you add, " . . . but your curiosity will compel you to do it." Do you want to say anything about that?

E: What is compelling? It's *her* curiosity. I'm not compelling her.

R: I see. You are evoking a compulsion within her but she can't blame it on you! You are utilizing her own inner compulsions. Fantastic! Next you continue with, "Over there in a chair about six feet away from you, when you develop enough courage, you will see yourself sitting there." What are you doing with that statement?

E: [Laughs] I have her hoping that what she'd see sitting there would be acceptable for her in that audience situation.

R: Why did you say, "when you develop enough courage"? Is your purpose to heighten her anxiety and expectancy again?

E: [Nods yes]

R: I thought it might be the opposite—a placing of the burden of the hallucination on her "when [she] develops the courage." It's like an implied directive. She doesn't have to look until she has the courage, but when she finally does look she *will* see it!

E: That gives her the *time* to develop the courage to develop a *safe* hallucination.

R: It allows time for the hallucinatory associations to come into play. You didn't just say, "Look over there and see yourself." That would have been very difficult to do.

E: She was sitting there, wearing a different skirt and blouse. She couldn't see herself in that evening's attire. [That is, she could not see herself wearing the same clothes in the hallucination as she was wearing in actuality.] That was over here. Sitting over there she'd have to be in another skirt and another blouse.

R: She says, "I am too sitting over there, but I am really sitting here, but I see myself sitting over there. . . . But that isn't possible." This is another level of awareness responding to you: consciously she realizes that she is experiencing a hallucination and says it isn't possible. This means that she is experiencing two levels of awareness: she experiences the hallucination on one level and criticizes it on another level. Then you add, "Even more astonishing will be the fact that you will see yourself standing behind the chair in which you are sitting." Why did you throw in this little bit?

E: A third skirt and a third blouse!

R: You're really interested in skirts and blouses?! Were you just trying to develop the hallucination further?

E: Yes, developing a hallucination further and letting *her* use *her own* knowledge of her wardrobe. . . . I was curious to see if she would follow the usual pattern.

R: What is the usual pattern?

E: Subjects don't hallucinate themselves in clothes they are wearing unless you give them instructions to do so.

R: That's interesting. It could be a subtle test for the validity of a visual hallucination.

Further Ratification of Genuine Hallucinatory Experience; Providing Lucid Explanations for Puzzling Trance Events

E: The class was invited to question her about the realities of the girl standing up, the girl sitting in that other chair, and the girl sitting in a chair beside the author. Her statement was simply, "That one standing up is really me. I know it is me. I know the girl sitting down in front of her is me, and I know that the I sitting right here is really me. But I also know there aren't three me's, but I do see them." With a trace of anxiety in her voice she turned to the author and asked, "How is this possible, because I know there aren't three me's yet I see them? How is this possible?"

The reply was given: "You really have nothing to be concerned about. *You are simply in a somnambulistic hypnotic trance and your visual memories of yourself have been vivified in the same fashion as you, in your dreams during sleep, vivify and make real your memories of other people, of various types of pleasures, of various life experiences.*"

She asked, "Am I really in a trance state?"

She was told, "Yes, you are, and I am using your services to demonstrate certain values of hypnotism to the class who, incidentally, you cannot see even though you know you are in a classroom." She looked toward the class and asked, "Did they go for a coffee break? I can see the chairs and the. . . . " [Thus ends this unfinished paper.]

Evoking Negative Visual Hallucinations; Memories and Associations as the "Magical" Determinants of Hallucinations

R: In this final section you evoke another hypnotic phenomenon indirectly. You make the class disappear such that a negative visual hallucination follows as an implication from your last comment. Here the manuscript ends. Do you have any memory of what happened after this?

E: I told her, "Now that was a negative visual hallucination. Would you like to call the class back? . . . Would you like to have your dinner?" She looked startled and said, "The whole class?" *The words aren't magical, memories are.*

R: Yes! Because your words are tripping off certain memories and associative processes which control her hallucinations.

E: That's *all* that's being controlled. You are dealing with *her*, with her capacities . . . and so forth.

R: This is a somnambulistic hypnotic trance. Yet she has to ask, "Am I in a trance?" Is that characteristic of somnambulistic behavior—that subjects do not know they are in a trance?

E: When you create multiple levels in consciousness, subjects don't know where they are.

R: They don't know where they are unless they find an ingenious way of testing it?

E: Haven't you had the experience of waking up in the morning in a strange place and, "Oh, what!?"

R: Yes, exactly. I just had that kind of experience a half-hour ago when Bernie came into the room and accidentally awakened me. I was in a trance and I thought I was in my office in Los Angeles. Then I realized, "Oh, no, I'm here in Phoenix!"

Capacities Required for Somnambulistic Behavior: Erickson's Versus Spiegel's View

R: Okay. Now, to cure my sense of inadequacy [about being able to facilitate hallucinations in my hypnotic subjects], I want to ask a question: Do you feel that the subject you described in this paper is an unusual person in her somnambulistic capacities? Or do you feel that by hitting the right associative processes, you should be able to do this with any subject?

E: With any intelligent subject! Just like this girl we saw earlier today [Miss X of Case 5 in Erickson & Rossi, 1979, pp. 143–234], and so was K. [K was a former patient who delighted Erickson because she was able to experience the somnambulistic phenomenon of being in "the middle of nowhere" or the "void," just as Erickson experienced it himself (Erickson & Rossi, 1977, p. 129). K was the patient we named "Mrs. A" in Erickson & Rossi, 1979, pp. 314–347.]

R: But do you believe like Dr. Spiegel that these subjects are what he calls "5's" [high hypnotic ability, Spiegel & Spiegel, 1978] and that somnambulism can be induced in only 10 to 20 percent of the population? Maybe only 10 or 20 percent of the population is intelligent enough?

E: No. . . .

V: Isn't it a matter of training? Cannot most people develop some of these capacities?

E: You couldn't possibly enable me to hallucinate music.

R: That's right. [Erickson frequently told anecdotes about his tone deafness and arrythmias (Erickson & Rossi, 1977).] So one way of preparing for any hypnotic phenomena, particularly hallucinatory behavior, is to begin activating associative processes even before you make the suggestion. That is one way. Heightening expectancy and anxiety is another general approach. What other factors are involved? Fixation of attention?

E: And narrowing of attention—

R: —to the area you want—to the visual memories used for visual hallucinations.

E: [An unclear portion of the audio tape in which Erickson gives an example of his daughter Kristina's *utilization* of a patient's desire to do what is right for health in order to get through an unpleasant medical examination.]

Utilization Theory of Hypnotic Phenomena

R: You tell the subject she is in a somnambulistic hypnotic trance "in the same fashion as you, in your dreams during sleep, vivify and make real your memories of other people, of various types of pleasures, of various life experiences." In this statement you are actually stating your theory of somnambulistic hypnotic trance. It is a reactivation of visual memories; you are utilizing the same mental mechanisms that are involved in dream states. This is your theory?

E: Yes. [Erickson explains how his approach with a city person would be different from his approach with a country person.] *But the subject produces [the hypnotic experience]. Your words are just to stimulate something in his head.*

R: That's right. The therapist's words stimulate and utilize processes within patients. Your words are not putting anything into patients; they are just stimuli tripping off programs already present in patients. *That is our utilization theory of hypnotic phenomena.*

E: [Nods his head yes with a broad grin and an apparent effort *not* to say anything for the audio recording]

V: That's his visual! [Everyone laughs]

R: [1984] Although Erickson introduced the concept of utilization for inducing hypnosis (Erickson, 1959), my efforts to generalize it into a *theory of hypnotic phenomena* may have seemed a bit pretentious and perhaps even laughable to Erickson. Like many enlightened teachers, he did not take his own concepts so seriously; he knew it was vastly more important to facilitate the process of learning itself rather than to promote his own tentative conclusions.

Discussion

Since Erickson's initial phrase of "hypnotic and nonhypnotic realities" identifies this unfinished fragment with his major paper on this theme (Erickson, 1967), we can use it as a guide for our discussion. We will use Erickson's own published words as much as possible to focus on his utilization approach to somnambulism and hallucinatory behavior.

1. *The hypnotic state is an experience that belongs to the subject.* In reviewing the history of his own developing understanding of hypnosis, Erickson (1967) focused on this element as follows:

> The above examples of totally unexpected, unplanned, and not understood experiences with hypnosis have been encountered many times in the author's career, and the cumulative effect has been to make the author ever-increasingly aware that the hypnotic state is an experience that belongs to the subject, derives from the subject's own accumulated learnings and memories, not necessarily consciously recognized but possible of manifestation in a special state of nonwaking awareness. Hence the hypnotic trance belongs only to the subject — the operator can do no more than learn how to proffer stimuli and suggestions that evoke responsive behavior based upon the subject's own experiential past. (pp. 42–43)

An appreciation of this understanding is fundamental in dealing with the major misconception that has plagued hypnosis since its beginning in ancient times: Hypnotic experience *seems* to result from the manipulative effect of an external agent (anything from planetary and human magnetisms to "prestige" and "influence communication"). The fact remains, however, that whenever hypnosis was rediscovered, it always occurred in the same manner: A "spontaneous" state of somnambulism was suddenly noticed in a subject. It was further noticed that this somnambulistic state, which had been initiated by spontaneous processes within the subject, could be guided or influenced to some small extent by talking to the subject (Boring, 1950). Erickson recounts this process of rediscovery with the fellow student he calls Miss O in his 1967 paper we quoted above. She surprised Erickson by "spontaneously" regressing to childhood when he inadvertently used the word *doggie* (instead of *dog*) with its childhood implications.

Every therapeutically oriented investigator since then has sought to utilize this spontaneous process initiated within the subject for "suggestion therapy." Thus, in the beginning of the modern era, Marquis de Puységur, a student of Mesmer's, named this state "artificial somnambulism" but naively believed that the subject was possessed of "second sight" and would follow "any" suggestion offered (Wolberg, 1948). Hypnosis continually fell into disrepute because these early naive beliefs involved exaggerations that were repeatedly disproven by the more critical and scientifically oriented investigators from academic environments.

The same problems of misunderstanding threaten us today as we once again attempt to capitalize on the findings and skills of Erickson as the most recent rediscoverer of the therapeutic possibilities of "artificial somnambulism." Even today we naively believe that we are putting people into a blank, impressionable "special" state and then "programming" them into health. There is a seed of truth in this naive view but only a seed. To nurture this seed, however, we really need to understand the full complexity of the situation. Erickson (1964, p. 15) explains it as follows:

> In general his findings, based upon experience with many thousands of subjects, have been that the simpler and more permissive and unobtrusive is the technique, the more effective it has proved to be, both experimentally and therapeutically, in the achievement of significant results. Also, his experience has been that the less the operator does and *the more he confidently and expectantly allows the subjects to do,* the easier and more effectively will the hypnotic state and hypnotic phenomena be elicited in accord with the subjects' own capabilities and uncolored by efforts to please the operator. However, it must be borne in mind that subjects differ as personalities, and that hypnotic techniques must be tailored to fit the individual needs and the needs of the specific situation. Therefore users of hypnosis should be fully cognizant with all types of hypnotic techniques and fully appreciative of the subjects as personalities. They should bear ever in mind that the role of the operator is no more than that of a source of intelligent guidance while the hyp-

notic subjects proceed with the work that demonstrates hypnotic phenomena, in-
sofar as is permitted by the subjects' own endowment of capacities to behave in
various ways.

2. *Deep trance experience involves a utilization of the subject's memories
of well-motivated life experiences* (in Erickson's words, "experiential learnings"). Erickson's pregnant phrase *"words aren't magical, memories are"* sums
up the essence of what he believes about how he facilitated the hallucinatory
behavior in this case. In his major paper on the utilization approach (1959)
he describes it as follows:

> These techniques are in essence no more than a simple reversal of the usual pro-
> cedure of inducing hypnosis. Ordinarily trance induction is based upon securing
> from the patients some form of initial acceptance and cooperation with the oper-
> ator. In Techniques of Utilization the usual procedure is reversed to an initial ac-
> ceptance of the patients' presenting behaviors and a ready cooperation by the
> operator however seemingly adverse the presenting behaviors may appear to be
> in the clinical situation. (p. 178)

To conclude his utilization paper (1959) Erickson writes:

> These methods are based upon the utilization of the subject's own attitudes,
> thinking, feeling, and behavior, and aspects of the reality situation, variously em-
> ployed, as the essential components of the trance induction procedure. In this way
> they differ from the more commonly used techniques which are based upon the
> suggestion of the subjects of some form of operator-selected responsive behavior.
> These special techniques, while readily adaptable to subjects in general, demonstrate
> particularly the applicability of hypnosis under various conditions of stress and
> to subjects seemingly not amenable to its use. They also serve to illustrate in part
> some of the fundamental psychological principles underlying hypnosis and its in-
> duction. (pp. 204–205)

3. *Erickson evokes and utilizes mental mechanisms to facilitate hypnotic
suggestion.* This seemingly simple statement actually describes the most subtle
element of Erickson's approach. The essence of his innovative contribution
lies in his evocation and utilization of mental mechanisms rather than the conventional process of analysis. Sigmund Freud was a genius of *analysis*; Jung
was a genius of *synthesis*; Erickson was a genius of *utilization*.

In the first hallucinatory experience of this case involving eating in a restaurant, Erickson demonstrates how he utilizes an initial negative mental set
(or the "resistance") to free an underlying cooperative wish for hypnotic experience. In facilitating the second hallucinatory experience wherein the subject sees three different images of herself, his commentaries reveal how he

was evoking and utilizing processes of surprise, curiosity, anxiety and inner compulsion, together with all the complex processes of real-life memories, to facilitate the visual hallucination. He did not simply put her in a somnambulistic state and directly suggest she see such-and-such. From Erickson's original and unfinished manuscript (and from many of his other publications), it sometimes seems as if he is making relatively direct suggestions. Only his commentaries reveal the actual complexity of his thinking about the underlying psychodynamics of the process.

The process of learning how to evoke and utilize patients' internal mental mechanisms, as well as the interpersonal dynamics of the hypnotic situation (Haley, 1963), is the major hurdle to becoming an Ericksonian hypnotherapist. Most of us who believe we are following Erickson are using *some aspects* of his approaches — but I have not yet seen anyone consistently demonstrate skill in all aspects of the utilization approach. Most of us know how to utilize the interpersonal level of the hypnotic process so ably presented by Haley (1963, 1982). However, I have not yet seen anyone demonstrate equal skill in evoking and utilizing the subject's internal mental mechanisms and memory, as Erickson does twice in this case illustration.

To my continuing personal chagrin, I must fully admit that I do not do this myself yet. I can share with you, though, how I am planning to learn. I am beginning to use what I believe is the clearest model of utilizing a subject's mental mechanisms that exists in the Ericksonian literature. This is the "reverse set" which Erickson demonstrated on film in 1958 at Stanford University for Hilgard and Haley. In the reverse set, Erickson systematically differentiates between the subject's "thinking and doing" to catapult her into "believing" she is in trance even while she is shaking her head that she is not. This example is presented and discussed in detail in *Experiencing Hypnosis* (Erickson & Rossi, 1981, pp. 154–178).

Why is it taking us so long to learn how to utilize rather than merely analyze internal processes? I believe it requires a new level of learning how to learn — a jump in "logical types," as Bateson calls it (1979). Bateson presents a brilliant and poignant example of this kind of learning as manifested by the dolphin. In Bateson's example, the dolphin's trainer wanted to demonstrate how he had "taught" the dolphin to perform a new trick — a new piece of behavior. Each time the dolphin came out to the demonstration pool in front of an audience, the trainer would wait until the dolphin "accidentally" did something new and would then reward it with food. When the dolphin came out for the next session, however, the trainer would not reward the piece of behavior the dolphin had been rewarded for in the previous session — the dolphin would simply perform it in vain. The trainer would not give any more food until a new piece of behavior emerged. Finally, as Bateson describes it:

In the time out between the fourteenth and fifteenth sessions, the dolphin appeared to be much excited; and when she came onstage for the fifteenth session, she put on an elaborate performance that included eight conspicuous pieces of behavior, of which four were new and never before observed in this species of animal. From the animal's point of view, there is a jump, a discontinuity, between logical types. (p. 123)

Would that we could be as such a dolphin!

References

BATESON, G. (1979). *Mind and nature*. New York: Dutton.

BORING, E. (1950). *A history of experimental psychology*. New York: Appleton-Century-Crofts.

ERICKSON, M. H. (1935). A study of an experimental neurosis hypnotically induced in a case of ejaculatio praecox. *The British Journal of Medical Psychology*, Part I, *15*. In E. L. Rossi (Ed.), *The collected papers of Milton H. Erickson on hypnosis*, Vol. III, 320–335.

ERICKSON, M. H. (1936). A clinical note on a word association test. *The Journal of Nervous and Mental Disease, 84*(5). In E. L. Rossi (Ed.), *The collected papers of Milton H. Erickson on hypnosis*, Vol. III, 289–291.

ERICKSON, M. H. (1944). The method employed to formulate a complex story for the introduction of an experimental neurosis in a hypnotic subject. *The Journal of General Psychology, 31*, 67–84. In E. L. Rossi (Ed.), *The collected papers of Milton H. Erickson on hypnosis*, Vol. III, 336–355.

ERICKSON, M. H. (1959). Further clinical techniques of hypnosis: Utilization techniques. *The American Journal of Clinical Hypnosis, 2*, 3–21. In E. L. Rossi (Ed.), *The collected papers of Milton H. Erickson on hypnosis*, Vol. I, 177–205.

ERICKSON, M. H. (1964). Initial experiments investigating the nature of hypnosis. *The American Journal of Clinical Hypnosis, 7*, 152–162. In E. L. Rossi (Ed.), *The collected papers of Milton H. Erickson on hypnosis*, Vol. I, 3–17.

ERICKSON, M. H. (1967). Further experimental investigation of hypnosis: Hypnotic and nonhypnotic realities. *The American Journal of Clinical Hypnosis, 10*, 87–135. In E. L. Rossi (Ed.), *The collected papers of Milton H. Erickson on hypnosis*, Vol. I, 18–82.

ERICKSON, M. H. (1980). Notes on minimal cues in vocal dynamics and memory. In E. L. Rossi (Ed.), *The collected papers of Milton H. Erickson on hypnosis*, Vol. I, 373–377.

ERICKSON, M. H. & ROSSI, E. L. (1977). Autohypnotic experiences of Milton H. Erickson. *The American Journal of Clinical Hypnosis, 20*, 36–54. In E. L. Rossi (Ed.), *The collected papers of Milton H. Erickson on hypnosis*, Vol. I, 108–132.

ERICKSON, M. H. & ROSSI, E. L. (1979). *Hypnotherapy: An exploratory casebook*. New York: Irvington.

ERICKSON, M. H. & ROSSI, E. L. (1981). *Experiencing hypnosis: Therapeutic approaches to altered states*. New York: Irvington.

HALEY, J. (1963). *Strategies of psychotherapy*. New York: Grune & Stratton.

HALEY, J. (1982). The contribution to therapy of Milton H. Erickson. In J. K. Zeig (Ed.), *Ericksonian approaches to hypnosis and psychotherapy*. New York: Brunner/Mazel.

HUSTON, P., SHAKOW, D., & ERICKSON, M. H. (1934). A study of hypnotically induced complexes by means of the Luria Technique. *The Journal of General Psychology, 11*, 65–97. In E. L. Rossi (Ed.), *The collected papers of Milton H. Erickson on hypnosis*, Vol. III, 292–319.

ROSSI, E. L. (Ed.). (1980). *The collected papers of Milton H. Erickson on hypnosis*. New York: Irvington. Volume I: *The nature of hypnosis and suggestion*. Volume II: *Hypnotic alteration of sensory, perceptual and psychophysiological processes*. Volume III: *Hypnotic investigation of psychodynamic processes*. Volume IV: *Innovative hypnotherapy*.

ROSSI, E., RYAN, M., & SHARP, F. (Eds.). (1983). *Healing in hypnosis: The seminars, workshops, and lectures of Milton H. Erickson*. (Vol. I). New York: Irvington.

SPIEGEL, H. & SPIEGEL, D. (1978). *Trance and treatment*. New York: Basic Books.

WOLBERG, L. (1948). *Medical hypnosis*. New York: Grune & Stratton.

Certain Principles
of Medical Hypnosis

Milton H. Erickson, M.D.

I believe that the average physician is mature and competent, and I am also convinced that his successful practice of medicine constitutes an adequate demonstration of his competency in dealing with and understanding adequately the psychodynamics of human behavior in stressful situations. I therefore suggest that we do not underestimate their capabilities as men with extensive training, both in school and in the field of experience.

In all of man's dealing with men, there is a need for the communication of ideas and understandings. And when man deals with man, as in the healing arts, communication is most important, since ideas and understandings affect in a multitude of ways the body's life processes. The recognition of the forces exerted by psychological behavior upon physiological responses is constantly growing, and this has reached the point at which medical science is demanding better and more effective ways of reordering psychological and physiological behavior disordered by various states of illness, emotion and misunderstandings. This is the reason for the current intense worldwide interest in hypnosis. Hypnosis is a scientific and effective methodology for the communication of ideas and understandings, for the eliciting of psychological and physiological responses conducive to the health and welfare of the individual, and for the educative procedures so needed in securing the cooperation of the afflicted.

Hypnosis is not a limited medical or dental or psychological specialty. Neither are there different kinds of hypnosis, such as psychiatric, dermatological, psychoanalytical, existential, psychodynamic, obstetrical, surgical, or asthmatic hypnosis. One does not use hypnosis on or for a disease, a pro-

*Dr. Erickson presented this paper at the 19th Congress of the Pan American Medical Association in Mexico City on May 4, 1960. The *Ericksonian Monographs* is indebted to Elizabeth M. Erickson for contributing this previously unpublished material.

Address reprint requests to: The Milton H. Erickson Foundation, Inc., 3606 North 24th St., Phoenix, AZ 85016.

cedure, or a condition. Instead, one employs hypnosis in relation to a patient and his needs and as a methodology remarkably useful in eliciting potentials of behavior and response existing within the patient but ordinarily overlooked and unused.

Hypnosis is, speaking simply, an effective clinical approach to the patient as a thinking, understanding and learning creature and it involves teaching the patient a better comprehension of himself and his capabilities as a functioning organism. It is not a matter of teaching a patient a school of interpretative thought and theory, such as the Freudian, the Adlerian or the Existentialist, as some would have you believe. These are but passing schools of thought that contribute here and there various items of knowledge, and then are replaced by new schools of thought.

Hypnosis is not a school of thought nor is it a theoretical interpretation of human behavior. Rather, hypnosis is a special state of conscious awareness, a special state of conscious awareness that has been in existence and daily manifested since the human race existed. Because it is a state of awareness, it has been hard to recognize and to define. There was a need for the development of psychology as a science to permit an open general recognition of hypnosis as a natural phenomenon of service to mankind in achieving an understanding of human functioning. Nevertheless, from the beginning of human history, hypnosis has been used blindly and unknowingly, with its progressive, intentional utilization dependent upon more adequate advances in other scientific areas involving an understanding of the basic principles of human behavior.

Now the time has arrived at which there is sufficient understanding of the complexities and varieties of human behavior to permit the utilization of hypnosis on a broader and more extensive basis for two immediate purposes: (1) the betterment of human welfare for the individual, and hence society; and (2) the development of research for a more adequate understanding of human capabilities and potentialities.

In this regard the question arises: In which way can hypnosis make these contributions? The answer, very simply, is that as a special state of conscious awareness, it makes possible a wealth of special forms of behavior and response, all based upon everyday normal experiences and learnings.

First of all, hypnosis allows a person as a personality to develop a state of objectivity ordinarily not possible, or most difficult to secure. In the field of psychiatry and in practically all fields of medicine, objectivity in viewing the self and meeting one's needs is of utmost importance and yet difficult to achieve. The patient in the hypnotic state can and does view the self with objectivity, with detachment, even dissociation, achieving an appraisal of his needs and capabilities ordinarily impossible. The utilization of this capability for objectivity is a most important technique in analyzing and securing an understanding of a patient's needs, and it offers opportunities not only for developing better clinical understandings but also opportunities for extensive research, particularly in the field of psychosomatic medicine, to name one area. Recognition of this objectivity is infinitely more important than describing hypnosis as a love relationship, or as a dependency relationship, as many psychoanalysts would have one believe.

Receptivity to ideas is another attribute of the hypnotic state that makes possible the communication to the patient of new and further understandings that might serve to educate or to reeducate him in accord with his needs but not the therapist's needs, as is so often the case with other therapeutic procedures. This receptivity is of special type, unique to hypnosis. It is a receptivity characterized by an exact reception of ideas without an elaboration of them in terms of implied or associated meanings. For example, if I were to ask somebody in the ordinary waking state, "Do you mind telling me your name?" the reply would be a courteous statement of his name. This response, however, would be one to the implication that his name was desired. The hypnotic subject, however, would be likely to reply with either a courteous affirmative or negative, but not by a response to the implications of the question. By virtue of this specific type of receptivity characteristic of hypnosis, the process of presenting ideas and understandings and effecting an education or a reeducation of the patient is greatly enhanced and accelerated.

Because of the combined effects of objectivity and specific receptiveness, a third item of behavior of marked significance in psychiatry, as well as other medical areas, becomes possible in the hypnotic state. This is the capacity to examine ideas for their inherent values, rather than in terms of prejudgments, opinions, mistaken beliefs, or faulty attitudes. For example, the 50-year-old man, asked in the ordinary waking state to describe his activities on his fourth birthday, can readily assert that they are forgotten and impossible to remember. The hypnotic subject readily appreciates the request as possible of response through the utilization of memory and association processes and he proceeds readily with the task as a reasonable and legitimate undertaking. This willingness to accept ideas in terms of intrinsic values constitutes the basic principle which makes it possible to call upon the patient to utilize the vast variety of learnings achieved through the experiential processes of life itself, whether they are conscious or unconscious, voluntary or involuntary, intentional or automatic. It is this basic characteristic of hypnotic behavior that allows or enables the patient in hypnosis to explore and to utilize the potentialities of his capacities to learn, to react, and to respond at all levels of functioning.

What I have said about hypnotic objectivity, receptivity and capacity to examine ideas and communications for their intrinsic values can also be said for other hypnotic phenomena.

Hypnotic dissociation is a most useful technique psychiatrically as well as in obstetrics and anesthesiology. Catalepsy, or balanced muscle tonicity, is of value in the psychological rehabilitation of the physically handicapped patient or the surgical patient needing immobility. Posthypnotic suggestion, based as it is upon participation, becomes the basis for even more participation by the patient in achieving his recovery.

I could go on giving the various applications for regression, revivification, ideomotor and ideosensory activities, amnesia, hypermnesia and for isolation phenomena, but I am confident that in your own scientific curiosity you yourselves will elaborate many new and valuable techniques of hypnosis applicable in all medical fields.

A States of Consciousness Model of Ericksonian Hypnosis

Stephen R. Lankton, M.S.W.

The interrelated fields of hypnotherapy, psychotherapy, and family therapy are experiencing a historical period of growth as a result of innovative techniques created by Milton H. Erickson, M.D. (1901–1980). His contributions are distinctive in many ways but are of special interest for the variety of treatments and interventions they provide. To explicate the uniqueness of his strategic approaches and interventions and increase their availability to hypnotherapists, this paper attempts to place them within a "states of consciousness" (SoC) model of mental processes. This is achieved by providing a guideline which traces the induction process in terms of the alternations in emphasis between conscious and unconscious SoCs. Finally, implications for family therapy are suggested.

Milton H. Erickson is recognized as the master of clinical hypnosis and strategic therapy. His influence has extended beyond dynamic techniques of intervention to reshape the very way we view clients and problems. This paper offers a States of Consciousness (SoC) perspective on clients and problems. Charles Tart produced a definitive essay concerning States of Consciousness (SoCs) as "a unique, dynamic pattern or configuration of psychological structures, an active system of psychological subsystems" (Tart, 1975, p. 5). He added that these states are held together or maintained by the loading of awareness/attention with stimuli provided by various tasks, chemicals, and so forth. That is, the stimulation provided by sensory and chemical inputs helps induce and continue a SoC. Once induced, they are maintained by feed-

Address reprint requests to: Stephen R. Lankton, M.S.W., P.O. Box 958, Gulf Breeze, FL 32561.

back created by mental monitoring (Tart, 1975, p. 5). In other words, each person does a self-observation that regulates the SoCs. Each SoC can be thought of as a different inner reality with different mental processes, muscle tonus, feelings, and associated actions. Examples are even noticed when a person claims, "I can't function very well yet because I haven't had my coffee," and "I'm not feeling like myself today so my judgment is a little off."

Since Ericksonian hypnosis provides a unique kind of interpersonal stimulation, it is well suited for producing and studying these inner realities. Erickson viewed trance as a state of consciousness in which certain associations were connected in a way that produced an inner "reality." This newly constructed reality expressed a creative recombination of previous learnings (Erickson & Rossi, 1979, p. 464). Those "previous learnings" were learnings that clients had gained in still other uncustomary states of consciousness. For example, in trance (a state of nonordinary consciousness), an adult presenting the problem of bulimia facilitated her cure by calling upon perceptions gained as a young girl when she was walking on a beach and experiencing a different uncustomary state of consciousness (Lankton & Lankton, 1983, pp. 179–184). In trance, a hysterical depression that prevented an adult from normal dating was solved through a reexamination of instructions acquired in childhood (Erickson & Kubie, 1980). These examples illustrate the empirical and therapeutic value in recognizing and utilizing various states of consciousness.

Although these states of consciousness exist "within" the individual, they are created by means of social interaction. Initially, they are created by the client's family (Laing, 1972); "the child is, in effect, hypnotized by his parents" (Berne, 1972, p. 343). In this sense, the concept of states of consciousness can be used as a means of integrating and understanding the interactional dynamics of individual and social experience.

Erickson's epistemological framework interrelates individual and social systems through the process of *intervention*. Because Erickson developed a method of *intervention* rather than a *theory of personality*, his students have been able to avoid those differences created by traditional *theories* of personality and family structure. Erickson's approaches achieved therapeutic impact at several levels of individual and social mental processes:

1. *unconscious* patterns of experience;
2. *conscious* beliefs and frames of reference;
3. *interpersonal* communication; and,
4. *family organization.*

Ericksonian method is based on the viewpoint that problems arise when clients become "stuck" in a SoC which lacks the resources needed to meet the social and behavioral demands confronting them. In some cases, the operative SoC might actually produce a maladaptive response. Erickson stated that "psychological problems exist precisely because the conscious mind does not know how to initiate psychological experience and behavior change to the degree that one would like" (Erickson & Rossi, 1979, p. 18). Instead of attempting to just remove symptoms, Erickson helped the client utilize and integrate unconscious resources (that usually existed outside the customary state of consciousness and belief system) to meet current life demands. He assumed that problems arose due to an inappropriate response to life's increasingly complex sanctions and role pressures. His therapy, therefore, often did not demand an immediate reduction in a symptom. Rather, his work centered on the development of needed resources. Often the conscious mind of the client would remain unaware of the scope of change so that new learnings did not constitute a threat to the customary state of consciousness.

Observing Erickson in action* led to the formulation of ideas about his work in terms of States of Consciousness (SoC). His contact with me helped me shape important attitudes and perceptions about people and their experiences that I use diagnostically. I found that certain ideas from the SoC concept helped me apply Erickson's interventions with both individuals and families in a systematic manner.

Ericksonian Hypnosis Stated in Premises Regarding SoC

I propose eight premises regarding SoC that can be used to bridge the gap between individual and family therapy and at the same time provide a schema for constructing *interlocking system-wide interventions* for use with any client system. I have used some identifying titles for these premises and I will deal with them individually: (1) requisite existence of states of consciousness; (2) resources and limits in different states; (3) functions of states of consciousness; (4) necessity of shifting between different states; (5) learned induction and maintenance of states of consciousness; (6) social induction and maintenance of SoCs; (7) rules regarding the recombining of experience; and (8) symptom formation and states of consciousness. These premises can help us conceive of a theoretical framework that accomplishes what Erickson's work demonstrated: implicit unity of individual and social systems and the creation of interventions that have a system-wide effect. Each premise will be examined first in relation to social systems dynamics, and then in relation to specific applications in clinical trance work.

---

*Personal contact, 1975–79, at 1201 Hayward, Phoenix, Arizona.

1. Shifts in States of Consciousness are a Fact of Human Life Manifested Socially or Culturally Via Rituals, Sanctions, and Rules of Conduct

People of every culture shift between various stages of consciousness throughout normal daily activities. Religious rituals, for example, are experienced differently from labor activities. In America, terms such as *work, weekends, vacation, prayer, studying, hanging out,* and so forth, denote more than different ways of structuring time; *each involves a recognizably different state of mind.* Cultural rituals constitute recorded rules concerning the methods for *"proper" induction and maintenance of consciousness.* The special words said at a marriage ceremony or during church prayer are examples. Another example is the conflict that arises if, while *hanging out,* an individual has thoughts about ambition and employment matters. Usually, speaking about these thoughts will result in a mild form of ridicule or punishment. Those thoughts are thus culturally controlled; certain mental states are expected to be in operation at certain times.

Many subtle aspects of culture can be seen as sanctions that guide conduct within different states of consciousness (Goffman, 1967; Laing, 1967; Pearce, 1974). These subtle aspects concern the "customary" hours for conducting business, proper social conduct, the length of a school hour, the duration of television broadcasts, highway speed limits, and even beliefs about the nature of "reality." The total effect of the direct and subtle regulation of consciousness is, in fact, the fabric of the culture. Rituals and rules of conduct are merely the outward manifestations.

2. Various SoCs Within the Individual Contain Discrete as Well as Overlapping Sets of Resources and Limitations. The Use or Misuse of These Sets Will Determine the Utility or Liability of any Particular SoC

Different states of conscious awareness are known as ego-states (Fenichel, 1945, p. 223) and, as such, involve a sense of awareness, identity, history, and specific social impact (Berne, 1966). For example, at times we act, think, and feel as we did as children and at times we act, think, and feel as our parents did (or might have in the situation). Other states of consciousness or unconsciousness may also be created in which some of these aspects may be changed or nonexistent. Whatever the case, in each particular state of consciousness certain resources or potentialities are available and certain limitations are imposed. Other resources and other limitations are found in other SoCs. Some resources and limiting experiences can be shared by several SoCs.

Throughout normal daily activities, an individual experiences some alterations of discrete states within the normal waking state. These alterations are
described in terms of moods, feelings, musings, daydreams, reflects, and so
forth. All are groupings of experience that allow for certain problem-solving
interactions with the environment. For example, feeling, thinking, and acting like a parent may be most useful when value judgments are necessary and,
likewise, a SoC that feels, thinks, and acts like a child is most appropriate
for meeting the social demands at parties. The use or misuse of these various alterations will determine whether or not a SoC functions as a resource
or a liability within a particular environment at any specific time.

3. The Function of Shifting SoCs if Problem Solving

Shifting SoCs makes it possible for a person to synthesize new combina-
tions of past experiences as needed in different life situations: It is the process that makes resource retrieval possible. A normal waking state of consciousness is composed of several discrete states of consciousness. Shifting
these discrete states is part of natural problem-solving activity for each individual. A particular SoC makes possible the use of specific sets of such functions. The example in the following section will further clarify this observation.

4. Shifting Between Different SoCs is Necessary for Optimal Survival, Creativity, and Intelligent Survival

People *must* alter their states of consciousness in order to interact with their
environments and each other in an effective and optimal manner. As an example, take the business person who solves a difficult problem on the tennis court.
The scenario usually goes like this: He or she has been unsuccessful solving
a problem after working hard for hours in a particular SoC (maintained by
caffeine and other stimuli from the office environment). Finally, he or she
goes out for an energetic game of tennis during which the answer is conceived.

States of consciousness are *induced* and *maintained* in conjunction with
the particular characteristics of each new context. Thus each SoC produces
an opportunity for a novel solution to a problem because the mentation and
mechanisms that operate within it organize experience in different ways.

5. Shifting and Altering States of Consciousness is Learned

The ability to alter and stabilize consciousness is learned. The learning can
occur on either conscious or unconscious levels, or a combination of both.
As with any other skill (e.g., playing piano, skating, penmanship, etc.), the

type of learning that occurs results in either efficacious or inefficient and inappropriate performance.

We expect that people would tend to induce and maintain the SoC they consider to be the most beneficial, prosperous, attractive, etc. Also, people will attempt to induce or maintain it in the best manner possible for them. A common example is found with individuals who complain that they "procrastinate." The illustration I use concerns the task of writing a dissertation. Often writers will complain that they do everything *except* sit down to write. They may decide to postpone writing (for just a moment) until they first clean the office, organize a bedroom drawer, take out the garbage, get a snack, read the paper, wash the windows, and so forth. Eventually, life demands take over and the time they might have used to write the dissertation has been squandered. This procrastination can be viewed as an induction ritual that is being used to prepare the SoC for writing. It could be speculated that the writer is using the lesser tasks to load his awareness with the stimuli that produce the SoC for mastery of the intended task. This is an example of the person doing his best to induce a SoC in the manner in which it was learned even when doing so is less effective than desired.

We can see this point again demonstrated in an example of pathological conduct involving child abuse. If, for instance, a child abuser finds most of the resources he needs in a SoC which is characteristically associated with certain levels of bodily tension, judgmental internal dialog, breathing patterns, voice tones, and so forth, he will select social and physical conditions that further maintain the SoC with those behaviors. Should he experience a zone of comfort normally associated with that SoC, he can be expected to apply those same behaviors even more intensely in an attempt to maintain the "world as he knows it." Thus the abuser may resort to shouting, striking, and abusiveness to maintain his unique problem-solving level of efficiency. His attempts to overemploy clumsy methods of maintenance will strain psychological mechanisms and lower the operational quality of his performance of social conduct. In other words, he may beat, shout, and abuse rather than discuss, listen, and negotiate. It can be seen that, in part, the function of some symptoms may be to continue the preferred SoC through lack of a better learned choice for control of conflict and tension. Finally, another type of symptom development results as the stressed physical and psychological mechanisms are chronically overused in this effort.

6. Social Stimuli Induce and Help Maintain SoCs

People use one another to help induce SoCs. This is true for even the "normal daily" SoC. Social systems (e.g., families) help maintain each member's preferred SoC and get other members to act so as to help maintain their own. Members maneuver other members into assisting the maintenance process.

Maneuvering can be done by agreeing on beliefs, rituals, and experiences, or it may be done by resorting to ulterior and defensive behavior (Berne, 1966; Goffman, 1967; Laing, 1967, 1970, 1972). Inductions of SoC are done by means of conscious, planfull maneuvers such as seduction, manipulation, courtship, child rearing, psychotherapy, hypnotherapy, and family therapy. In contrast to these consciously deliberate methods, it is also done by means of unconscious automatic strategies such as defenses and repetitive "game" sequences, as well as by means of ordinary daily transactions.

> In the family situation, however, the hypnotist (the parents) are already hypnotized (by their parents) and are carrying out their instructions, by bringing their children up to bring their children up . . . in such a way, which includes not realizing that one is carrying out instructions, since one instruction is not to think that one is thus instructed. (Laing, 1972, p. 79)

7. Recombining and Shifting Experience Within SoCs is Rule-Governed

There is a saying that: "You can't get there from here." This is also true for mental processes: Some mental processes are directly interconnected while others are not. It may be easy to switch from Set A to Set B, but impossible to go from Set A to Set M. For example, a person may be able to go from *wondering* to *self-doubting*, but it is unlikely he or she could switch directly from *self-doubting* to *joy* even though these may all be normal waking state experiences for the person.

"Rules of recombining" different SoCs for each individual vary greatly. The verbally abusive man who can't smile and apologize during an angry exchange may be able to smile during other circumstances. But within his normal state of consciousness, rules of recombining prevent him from a verbal altercation with the display of a smile. He may have learned no way to get from *tension* to *smiling* in a social situation. In a further example is the common situation where two family members are quarreling and, in the heat of the exchange, one of them is able to answer a ringing telephone and sound pleasant. The other family member cannot. One might say there are no "roads" in his or her "map of experience" from argumentative behaviors to pleasant behaviors. The rules of recombining are idiosyncratic for each individual.

8. Symptom Formation Results from a Misuse of SoCs

The inability to maintain a SoC and shift among appropriate SoCs creates stress. Moments of stress invite an overuse or misuse of maintenance mechanisms or resources available in any given SoC which results in symptomatology. An example of this process is the stress that occurs with sleep deprivation. It is well known that the misuse of caffeine or other chemicals as a means of maintaining a waking state will produce various short-term symptoms ranging from irritability to paranoia.

The development of symptoms in a family member often serves the function of evoking and maintaining otherwise unstable SoCs among other family members. In extremely rigid family systems, the emergence of symptomatic behavior is a highly symbolic unconscious product of such "transpersonal collusion" (Laing, 1972, p. 99). An example of this conduct is seen when a child develops a school phobia and the anxieties of the parents are displaced as concern for the youngster. The more rigid the family system, the more the symptom localized in a single individual will serve as a metaphoric statement of the family stress.

Ericksonian Approach to Induction

Thus far we have looked at individual and family systems in terms of a SoC model. Now we will examine these aspects that relate to Erickson's work with hypnosis and families. Having presented the premises derived from my study with Erickson* in terms of a SoC model, we can now examine how shifts in states of consciousness (SoC) occur during clinical trance.

Erickson considered hypnotic trance to be a state of heightened, internally concentrated awareness that had its less specialized correlate in the form of the "common everyday trance" (Erickson & Rossi, 1979) which most people experience intermittently as a matter of course throughout the normal daily cycle of shifts in consciousness. Erickson conceptualized hypnosis as a state of consciousness in which *ideas* were better communicated and exchanged in a manner superior to normal waking state consciousness. Erickson used indirect forms of communication as a means of stimulating creative, independent thinking in his clients. His multileveled suggestions would constellate networks of associations that culminated in a cohesive, unified trance experience. Erickson and Rossi (1979) commented on this phenomenon:

> Associating suggestions in such interlocking chains creates a network of mutually reinforcing directives that gradually form a new self-consistent inner reality called "trance." It is construction of such interlocking networks of associations that gives "body" or substance to trance as an altered state of consciousness with its own guideposts, rules, and "reality." (p. 464)

---

*These premises are the conclusions from numerous personal observations of Erickson's work that initiated my understanding of each of the premises. The scope of the present article makes it impossible to describe all these observations.

The net result of these many associations may be experienced consciously to varying degrees. Much of the therapeutic process, however, remains unconscious in the normal waking state. In either case, the unconscious associations create the therapeutic basis of the trance that results. But, the induction of the trance state is the first important step.

Tracing the Induction Process

The following guidelines* have been particularly useful for tracing the induction process. They reflect the change in *emphasis* Erickson often evoked in states of conscious and unconscious processes during a hypnotic induction. The actual steps of induction overlap extensively, and there is no artificial break in the stages as implied in this guideline. Major shifts in emphasis can be traced through these stages:

1. *Orienting the client to trance.* The goal of this first phase is to find a natural method to relax the client's normal waking-state conscious. This is accomplished by ensuring that the client is physically and psychologically prepared for trance. Part of the preparation involves identifying and dispelling myths the client may hold concerning hypnosis. To facilitate this phase, the Ericksonian therapist often uses stories that demonstrate the common experience of trance on both personal and cultural levels. Observations will be shared of cultural and personal behavior upon which the first several premises were formulated. These often include: the requisite existence of states of consciousness, resources and limits existing in different states, the function of states of consciousness, and the necessity of shifting between different states for problem solving. The therapist might say, for example, "Everyone knows how to daydream," "Sooner or later everyone drops into a trance and examines things from a different angle," "Every child knows the importance of imagining and the value of wonder," "It is important to forget things now and then," and so forth.

To the extent that education of the client involves the use of stories from the therapist's life or evokes memories from the client, a fixation of attention is initiated and step one is essentially complete.

2. *Fixating attention and rapport.* The goal at this phase is to disrupt the customary waking SoC by attaching the client's attention onto a story, body sensations, or an external object. The reader will recall that there is an "in-

---

*A more extensive discussion of this outline can be found in S. Lankton and C. Lankton, *The Answer Within: A Clinical Framework of Ericksonian Hypnotherapy,* 1983, Brunner/Mazel, pp. 131–177.

ducing" force from outside stimuli and from the client's conscious feedback and that this maintains his or her normal waking state.

While classical hypnotic approaches fixate attention on the goal of relaxation, the Ericksonian approach recognizes that many individuals *struggle* to achieve relaxation and in so doing, actually *increase* the stability of their waking state. This struggle against relaxation (or giving up other familiar patterns of behavior), in fact, prevents many people from going into trance with "classical" induction techniques (Spiegel, 1972). An important aspect of Erickson's therapeutic contribution was his development of the *utilization approaches* to hypnotic induction whereby *any* presenting behavior is accepted and utilized as a trance-inducing agent (Erickson, 1980c, pp. 177–205). The importance of the utilization approach is underscored here as the basis for assuming that most individuals can experience trance.

For example, when Erickson told the compulsive pacer to pace the floor even more, the client's usual SoC was no longer applicable. The tension of his customary interpersonal role was dispelled. He was no longer at the mercy of the usual maintenance control created by verbal struggle with those who encouraged him to relax nor did he have the bodily struggle that ensued when he attempted to relax. The client's habitual social and cognitive role became the object of his observation rather than object for struggle. Thus, his customary SoC reality perceptions and conscious beliefs were not reinforced *vis à vis* his struggle with a hypnotist demanding or encouraging that he relax.

3. *Dissociating conscious and unconscious processes.* The next major goal is to create a state in which the client's attention is dissociated and polarized by using language that contrasts the functioning of conscious and unconscious processes in a way that the client can understand. Again, this involves indirect techniques including the use of anecdote and metaphor, to direct and educate the client about the functioning of unconscious thought processes. In order to illustrate I will present a portion of an actual induction.

> There are a number of ways you can go about altering your state of consciousness. You might even open your eyes while in the trance and check out the room, and close them again. Realize that you put yourself in trance by stimulating mechanisms that are known to you. Your conscious mind's probably not likely to be able to articulate what those are but your unconscious can use them nonetheless. Your conscious mind may be attempting to have no thoughts to concentrate but your unconscious will still synthesize experience in a unique way. And your conscious mind might think you can create a situation similar to previous trance but your unconscious is more than likely creating a unique synthesis that reflects this particular moment. Sooner or later your conscious mind will seize upon an idea or an image. It will be interesting if that's the same as what your unconscious will be sorting through. Usually your conscious mind begins a line of thought and your

unconscious will continue the line of thought to its culmination. That way your conscious mind is free to skip to a new idea. It really would be difficult for a person to say whether or not the next idea chosen by the conscious mind is simply an epiphenomenon of your unconscious experience. You might prefer to think that your unconscious experience is guided by a sequence of willfully chosen conscious thoughts. You certainly can willfully focus your mind on one of your hands. It appears that your right hand has a general sense of catalepsy and dissociation that it already displays. To a lesser degree, so does your left hand.*

As this example shows, educating the client's customary SoC about the functioning of aspects of other (unconscious) SoCs creates a duality of thought and begins to sensitize the client to ongoing differences between conscious and unconscious mental processes. It is desirable if this results in a splitting of attention and creates two effects at once. First, it weakens the integrity of the rigidly held conscious waking state beliefs by involving the client in phenomena that are occurring beyond the limited scope of normal waking consciousness. Observing the previously unnoticed associations and processes that accompany trance requires the client to seek a new framework that will give meaning to them. In the example above this may be most apparent where the therapist guided the client to notice how an idea is seized and to notice a growing dissociation in his hands. Clients will attempt to employ previously held attitudes about what hypnosis ought to be in order to make this integration. Since the Ericksonian therapist holds the premise that experiences in other SoCs can be utilized as beneficial resources, he or she supports and guides the client in formulating a favorable view of unconscious potential. In operational terms, the guidance may be as subtle as saying, as in the example, that the unconscious synthesizes ideas and carries out thoughts. This implies an active and ambitious quality. Or, in other cases, it may be more explicit, as in, "I wonder if you are aware that your unconscious can work with comfort and ease?"

The second effect of creating dual conscious and unconscious mental processes is achieved to the extent that awareness is focused on nonordinary (to the customary SoC) experiences. When the therapist selects the experiences and focuses awareness in this manner, the interaction serves to structure the fabric of the induced SoC and "give substance" (Erickson & Rossi, 1979) to the trance state. This brings the therapist to the final step in the induction: drawing together and stabilizing the elements of the nonordinary SoC into an experience of therapeutic trance.

---

*This is an excerpt from an induction done by the author at a workshop, August 3–12, 1984 in Albuquerque, NM.

4. *Ratifying and deepening the trance.* Ratification of trance involves gaining clients' understanding of the fact that they have achieved a nonordinary SoC that can be used for therapeutic purposes. This is easily accomplished by focusing awareness on the many alterations that have occurred in facial muscles, reflexes, respiration, and so forth. As ratification "sinks in," a feedback loop is created whereby clients begin sustaining the trance state on their own. At the ratification stage, clients have placed their awareness on their own internal processes and their consciousness has been educated and oriented toward a positive problem-solving frame.

Let us look at one simple example. If the therapist has suggested the dissociation and levitation of the right hand but the client has levitated the left hand, the situation can go as follows: The therapist points out to the client that not lifting the hand that was suggested indicates that he or she does not follow "irrelevant suggestions." The implication is that the levitation is what is meaningful, while the handedness is inconsequential. Further, the lifting of the left hand indicates that nonordinary processes are occurring, whereas a lifting of the suggested right hand would indicate a less special response. Thus, the client has the nonordinary experience of his or her hand levitating, which in turn inclines the client to further monitor such instances. Thus clients can place attention/awareness on how they are following only relevant suggestions, and a feedback mechanism is set in operation. Also, clients monitor how much nonordinary processing is occurring, which in turn, operates as another client-conducted feedback loop helping to maintain the trance.

Trance deepening may be facilitated by the presentation of several types of techniques (the confusion technique, indirect suggestions, binds, and so forth) aimed at increasing the noticeability of nonordinary processes. If awareness for the novel processes increases and residual monitoring of the customary SoC decreases, then clients will be able to sustain their own trances. Otherwise, the therapist must provide the stimulation that focuses the client's awareness to maintain the trance state. At this point in the process the therapist can now turn most of his or her attention to the actual therapy that will be carried out in the trance state.

5. *Using trance to elicit and associate experiences.* Although this article deals primarily with the *induction* of SoCs, perhaps a few words on the *therapeutic process within trance* are in order. In the same manner that Erickson utilized subsystems of noncustomary SoCs to induce trance, his hypnotherapy also involved the use of these same mechanisms. He might, for example, use the mental mechanism of memorization of multiplication tables to help clients more thoroughly learn a feeling of self-worth within trance. That is, clients could more systematically examine the experience of self-worth by applying the method of scrutiny that was learned in the activity of memorization.

Once an altered SoC is established, experience from other SoCs can be incorporated into the trance. Determination of which experiences are needed is suggested by the diagnostic assessment and the contracted therapy goals. The needed experiences are often elicited with indirect suggestion, anecdotes, binds, and metaphors which provide an altered frame of reference that stimulates clients to entertain the possibility of — or the reality of — novel experience. Finally, the elicited experiences are arranged into a network of associations that help clients form a new "map of conduct" derived from a recombination of past perceptual, emotional, and behavioral patterns. Although the outcome of these changes will be known in part to the conscious mind in the normal waking state, it is not possible or necessary to know all of the new changes in the "map." By analogy, when new roads are built in a city, it is not necessary for the citizens to know all of the pillars and supports, nor even all of the destinations that can be reached by the new structures. It is sufficient for them to know how to get where they want and need to go.

When the associations are made and sufficiently reinforced for the session, the trance can end. It should be emphasized that the Ericksonian approach *does not* rely upon direct suggestions aimed at reducing the symptom. Instead, it aims at building resources by which the "whole" person can become equipped to handle the demands that may have created the context within which the symptom developed. Since symptoms are a signal that an individual or family is responding in a limited way to the strains being placed on exiting SoCs, treatment is a matter of bringing necessary outside resources into the customary SoC.

6. *Reorienting the client to waking state.* Whether reorientation is rapid or gradual, it resolves the temporary suspension of the normal waking state. At this stage the therapist has a final opportunity to assist clients in developing amnesia, posthypnotic behavior, and/or other trance phenomena that may be part of the treatment plan. Determination of the proper *therapeutic* arrangement for reorientation may be a complex matter (Lankton & Lankton, 1983).

The actual reorientation of *consciousness* is, by contrast, rather easy. Once the client's attention/awareness is directed away from the trance experience, with the therapist reinforcing the shift in direction, the habitual mechanism that creates the normal waking state will reassemble. The client will begin to feel "normal" again but this customary SoC will perhaps have some new perceptions within its familiar boundaries: These will be the learnings that were gained in the trance and partly or fully brought back into the conscious waking state under the hypnotist's guidance. Of course, the Ericksonian therapist will be cautious to provide necessary explanations and positive frames for the customary SoC to interpret any potentially hurtful material that is being integrated from noncustomary SoCs.

Implications for a SoC Model
of Family Therapy

As the influence of Erickson's work becomes increasingly appreciated, his techniques become more frequently used and the opportunity arises for development of a unifying theory. The increased use of his approach is stimulating an integration between the induction of the clinical SoC and the function of family systems. Erickson's major departure from classical hypnosis involved his technique of retrieving resources from SoCs that could be used to induce trance adequately (even creatively). These same resources would now be available for therapeutic use in the client's normal waking state. This paper has attempted to unite those aspects of Erickson's approach that deal with individual and social functioning under the rubric of "states of consciousness," and to demystify the mechanics of trance induction via the reformulation of it in terms of a SoC model.

Trance phenomena in family therapy and family life, "common everyday trance" experience (Erickson & Rossi, 1981, p. 48), and the therapeutic employment of states of consciousness are similarly becoming demystified and unified into a variety of clinical settings (Ritterman, 1983; Lankton & Lankton, 1983). The analysis provided in this paper primarily applies to the therapeutic use of hypnotherapy with individuals but the same principles also can be applied to Ericksonian work with families.

We have seen how therapists can help to induce new SoCs out of current consciousness. A further analysis could show how these same principles are unwittingly followed by parents as they hypnotize their children. One might easily see how, in family therapy, the use of paradoxical prescriptions and the refusal to play the expected role in the family drama would parallel the fixation phase of the induction process described above. A strong connection between this analysis and the dynamics of family therapy will be the subject of a subsequent writing (Lankton & Lankton, in press).

Conclusion

For now, the author has sought to demonstrate Ericksonian principles of therapy within a SoC model. This paper analyzes a typical form of Ericksonian induction and relates that analysis to eight premises about SoC. In so doing it hopes to provide a bridge between the seemingly divergent fields of hypnotherapy and family therapy. Understanding the function and effect of Ericksonian interventions on the varying and shifting states of consciousness that shape experience can help therapists achieve a more natural, accurate, and efficacious application, and hopefully can also help researchers design and implement increasingly scientific studies of these techniques.

References

BERNE, E. (1966). *Principles of group treatment*. New York: Grove.

BERNE, E. (1972). *What do you say after you say hello?* New York: Grove.

BROWN, D. P. & FROMM, E. (1977). Selected bibliography of readings in altered states of consciousness (ASC) in normal individuals. *International Journal of Clinical & Experimental Hypnosis, 25*, 338–391.

ERICKSON, M. H. (1980a). Initial experiments investigating the nature of hypnosis. In E. L. Rossi (Ed.), *The collected papers of Milton H. Erickson on hypnosis: Vol. 1. The nature of hypnosis and suggestion* (pp. 3–17). New York: Irvington.

ERICKSON, M. H. (1980b). A special inquiry with Aldous Huxley into the nature and character of various states of consciousness. In E. L. Rossi (Ed.), *The collected papers of Milton H. Erickson on hypnosis: Vol. 1. The nature of hypnosis and suggestion* (pp. 83–107). New York: Irvington.

ERICKSON, M. H. (1980c). Further clinical techniques of hypnosis: Utilization techniques. In E. L. Rossi (Ed.), *The collected papers of Milton H. Erickson on hypnosis: Vol. 1. The nature of hypnosis and suggestion* (pp. 177–205). New York: Irvington.

ERICKSON, M. H. (1980d). Hypnotism. In E. L. Rossi (Ed.), *The collected papers of Milton H. Erickson on hypnosis: Vol. 3. Hypnotic investigation of psychodynamic processes* (pp. 21–26). New York: Irvington.

ERICKSON, M. H. (1980e). Hypnotic psychotherapy. In E. L. Rossi (Ed.), *The collected papers of Milton H. Erickson on hypnosis: Vol. 4. Innovative hypnotherapy* (pp. 35–48). New York: Irvington.

ERICKSON, M. H. & KUBIE, L. S. (1980). The successful treatment of a case of acute hysterical depression by a return under hypnosis to a critical phase of childhood. In E. L. Rossi (Ed.), *The collected papers of Milton H. Erickson on hypnosis: Vol. 3. Hypnotic investigation of psychodynamic processes* (pp. 122–142). New York: Irvington.

ERICKSON, M. H. & ROSSI, E. L. (1979). *Hypnotherapy*. New York: Irvington.

ERICKSON, M. H. & ROSSI, E. L. (1980). Autohypnotic experiences of Milton H. Erickson. In E. L. Rossi (Ed.), *The collected papers of Milton H. Erickson on hypnosis: Vol. 1. The nature of hypnosis and suggestion* (pp. 108–132). New York: Irvington.

ERICKSON, M. H. & ROSSI, E. L. (1980). The varieties of double bind. In E. L. Rossi (Ed.), *The collected papers of Milton H. Erickson on hypnosis: Vol. 1. The nature of hypnosis and suggestion* (pp. 412–429). New York: Irvington.

ERICKSON, M. H. & ROSSI, E. L. (1980). The indirect forms of suggestion. In E. L. Rossi (Ed.), *The collected papers of Milton H. Erickson on hypnosis: Vol. 1. The nature of hypnosis and suggestion* (pp. 452–477). New York: Irvington.

ERICKSON, M. H. & ROSSI, E. L. (1981). *Experiencing hypnosis: Therapeutic approaches to altered states*. New York: Irvington.

ERICKSON, M. H., ROSSI, E. L., & ROSSI, S. I. (1976). *Hypnotic realities. The induction of clinical hypnosis and forms of indirect suggestion*. New York: Irvington.

FENICHEL, O. (1945). *The psychoanalytic theory of neurosis.* New York: Norton.

GOFFMAN, E. (1967). *Interaction rituals.* Chicago: Doubleday.

HUXLEY, A. (1956). *The doors of perception and heaven and hell.* New York: Harper & Row.

JUHASZ, J. B. (1979). Theories of hypnosis and theories of imagining. *Academic Psychology Bulletin, 1*(2), 119–128.

LAING, R. D. (1967). *The politics of experience.* New York: Ballantine.

LAING, R. D. (1970). *Knots.* New York: Random House.

LAING, R. D. (1972). *Politics of the family and other essays.* New York: Random House.

LANKTON, S. R. (1985). Multiple embedded metaphor. In J. K. Zeig (Ed.), *Ericksonian psychotherapy, Vol. 1: Structures* (pp. 171–195). New York: Brunner/Mazel.

LANKTON, S. R. & LANKTON, C. H. (1983). *The answer within.* New York: Brunner/Mazel.

LANKTON, S. R. & LANKTON, C. H. (in press). *Enchantment and intervention in the family: A framework of Ericksonian family therapy.* New York: Brunner/Mazel.

McCABE, M. P. (1978). Hypnosis as an altered state of consciousness: I. A review of traditional theories. *Australian Journal of Clinical Hypnosis, 6,* 39–54.

MORGAN, A. & HILGARD, J. (1978). The Stanford hypnotic susceptibility scale for adults. *American Journal of Clinical Hypnosis, 21,* 148–169.

PEARCE, J. C. (1974). *Exploring the crack in the cosmic egg.* New York: Simon & Schuster.

RITTERMAN, M. (1983). *Using hypnosis in family therapy.* San Francisco: Jossey-Bass.

ROGERS, C. R. (1961). *On becoming a person.* Boston: Houghton-Mifflin.

SHOR, R. E. (1972). Three dimensions of hypnotic depth. In C. T. Tart (Ed.), *Altered states of consciousness* (pp. 257–267). New York: Doubleday.

SPIEGEL, H. (1972). Eye roll test for hypnotizability. *American Journal of Clinical Hypnosis, 15,* 25–28.

TART, C. T. (1975). *States of consciousness.* New York: Dutton.

A Cybernetic Model
of Ericksonian Hypnotherapy:
One Hand Draws the Other

William J. Matthews, Ph.D.

The work of Milton Erickson has long been associated with the North American school of strategic therapy. This view takes a pragmatic or "what works" approach to psychotherapy and deemphasizes the value of theory in clinical practice. Clinical practice separated from theory can lead to the arbitrary application of technique and possible harm to the client. The purpose of this paper is twofold: (1) to underscore the important mutual relationship between theory and practice; and (2) to present a cybernetic or recursive model of Ericksonian hypnotherapy. A cybernetic perspective emphasizes the mutually influencing client-therapist *relationship* rather than viewing the therapist as independent from the client's behavior. Specifically, the interactions of the therapist-client system in relationship to diagnosis, treatment goals, and Ericksonian treatment interventions such as utilization, indirection, hypnosis, and metaphor are presented within a cybernetic model.

Erickson's work is associated with a pragmatic or utilitarian approach to change (Mackinnon, 1983), but it can be considered from an aesthetic theoretical base. When it is, it expands the range of interaction on the part of the therapist and enriches the relationship between the client and therapist. A utilitarian or pragmatic approach focuses on "what works" in therapy. In contrast, an aesthetic theory recognizes the complexity in human interaction and seeks to uncover the patterns that connect the individual to his or her social

Address reprint requests to: William J. Matthews, Ph.D., Assistant Professor, Counseling Psychology Program, Hills South, University of Massachusetts, Amherst, MA 01003.

The author would like to express his sincere appreciation to Stephen Lankton, A.C.S.W., for his helpful suggestions in the revision of this manuscript.

network. The analogy is to the musician with superb technique who can play notes but fails to grasp the melody and the clinician with great clinical technique who fails to appreciate the larger system in which he or she and the client operate. Pragmatic/intervention and aesthetic/theory form an important complementary relationship. The purpose of this paper is to provide a theoretical framework for Ericksonian hypnotherapy in which the aesthetic connections between the therapist and client are considered in a mutually influencing circular or recursive system of interaction.

Perhaps because Erickson did not operate from a formal theory of personality (Lankton & Lankton, 1983; Erickson & Rossi, 1980), his work is best considered from a pragmatic perspective. There is a potential problem in a purely pragmatic approach. It is that the therapist may view him- or herself as controlling the client and thereby causing the client to change. The notion of causality and control by the therapist separates therapy from its social and interactional context (as if the client exists in a vacuum). The Milan approach (Selvini-Palazzoli, Boscolo, Cecchin, & Prata, 1980) with its emphasis on systemic thinking and search for the patterns that connect family members is an aesthetically-oriented therapy, while the Haley and M.R.I. approaches are pragmatic. The differences between the two approaches are the underlying premises and the role taken by the therapist. Considering Erickson's work from only a view of "what works" is unnecessarily limiting and only partially descriptive of his approach and can lead to misapplication of Ericksonian techniques.

There is a temptation to believe that because Erickson espoused no formal theory of therapy, no theory is needed. However, theory, whether explicit or implicit, underlies all clinical practice. Clinical technique cannot exist in a vacuum. Prior to the presentation of a recursive model of Ericksonian therapy (i.e., a model in which the therapist and client form a mutually influencing or circular relationship), I will briefly discuss the value of theory in clinical practice.

The Importance of Theory in Clinical Practice

A number of authors (e.g., Erickson & Rossi, 1980; Haley, 1978; Laing, 1972; Szasz, 1974; Whitaker, 1976) have indicated that theory can be an impediment to clinical practice. In summary, their view is that a theory can be unnecessarily limiting to the clinician. The clinician who steadfastly adheres to a particular theory has blinders and may not perceive or conceive actions that could have therapeutic value for the client. There are many more clinicians who eschew theory altogether and pick from a smorgasbord of clinical techniques in order to promote therapeutic change with their clients. However, as Keeney & Sprenkle (1982) indicated, either of these two positions can lead the clinician to overlook the connection between theory and practice and the importance of the relationship between the two.

Even the clinician who uses technique to the conscious exclusion of theory must operate with some theory of how one knows the world around him or her. That theory is a part of the therapist's epistemology. However, while every therapist has a unique epistemological perspective, it does not follow that she or he is aware of the connection between that theory and the therapy she or he conducts. Keeney and Sprenkle (1982) indicated that all strategies of action have inherent theory that, in part, generate one's actions. Furthermore, actions contribute to the formation of theory. This mutually influencing process between theory and action can be called a "recursive" relationship. A recursive relationship focuses on the circular organization of events rather than on any particular linear sequence (Keeney, 1983, p. 19).

Bateson (1972) was particularly concerned with the willingness of many clinicians to ignore the connection between theory and practice and plunge impulsively toward therapeutic action. He indicated that action, devoid of aesthetic consideration, could lead to the frustration of the therapist (i.e., that he or she cannot *cause* the desired change to occur) and/or harm to the client (an exacerbation of the symptomatic behavior because more of the same wrong interventions are used). This is not to suggest that the clinician should never attempt new actions in the absence of theoretical support but rather therapists should consider the simultaneous and recursive influence of theory and practice. Each expands and supports the other.

Cybernetics and Therapy

Having derived an understanding of the "recursive relationship" between theory and practice, let us examine the relationship between cybernetics and the process of therapy. Keeney defines cybernetics as "the science of pattern and organization which is distinct from any search for material, things, force, and energy" (1983, p. 61). We could say that cybernetics is a paradigmatic leap from the universe of material objects to the study of the patterns of relationships *between* objects. Ecologists and biologists, for instance, in recognizing the interdependence of plants and animals, have long noted the importance of the *relationship* between species rather than considering the species in isolation. The predator-prey relationship maintains the balance of a given ecology. For example, deer allowed to proliferate and graze in the absence of a predator, eventually destroy food supplies and thereby affect other species living in that ecological niche. In the absence of self-correcting feedback (e.g., the predator-prey relationship), a system can break down.

Self-corrective feedback is the essential concept of cybernetics. Keeney (1983) described it as a process by which information proceeds backward from an act to reorganize whatever pattern (e.g., muscles, thoughts and/or interpersonal interactions) which regulated a performance. A thermostat is an example of a simple cybernetic process in which heat is regulated by the continuous fluctuations of the thermostat in a self-corrective process. In this feedback process, change and fluctuation of the thermostat maintain the stability of the temperature in the room. In therapy, a family or an individual client may show a great deal of change at one level in the system in order to maintain stability at another level in the system. For example, children continually undergo developmental changes while the stability of the family system is typically maintained. Change and stability in families are analogous to the predator and prey relationship in biology. They form a cybernetic complementarity. One does not exist in the absence of the other.

Let us look at an example of the change-stability cycle in clinical practice. One of my clients complained of having panic attacks when leaving the home. To intervene only at the level of the client's complaint ignores the social context. One hypothesis was that the client's panic attacks (changes in behavior) regulated her relationship with her husband and her mother (higher order stability in the system). A panic attack allowed the husband to attend to his wife's needs and yet limit his closeness to her. Also, the wife could assert herself in her home with her mother (when she could not leave, she took more charge in the home). This increased assertion may have inhibited conflict between the husband and an intrusive mother-in-law.

Effective therapy in this situation required feedback that would change the recursive pattern connecting the client, family, and therapist (Keeney, 1983). The pattern of feedback that maintains the client's specific panic behavior (e.g., riding in the car towards a shopping center, changes in respiration and heart rate, approaching a store, increasing sense of aloneness, etc.) as well as the higher order feedback (i.e., the relationship between the client, husband and her mother) must be determined. The therapist is presented with information from various levels within the client system which support both change and stability (i.e., "change the client so we the family will stay the same"). The therapist should consider at what level an intervention will be most effective, recognizing that he or she has become part of the system in which the client interacts and therefore may be a part of the feedback loop that helps maintain the symptomatic behavior. If therapy were to intervene only at the client's specific behavioral level to the exclusion of the social context, then the therapist may be helping to maintain the stability of the larger system, in which case the panic attacks are unlikely to subside.

In the above example, an attempt by the client to leave home would evoke the panic attack which maintains the client's anxiety. The higher order process is the pattern of relationships between the client, her husband, and her mother. The goal of therapy is to activate the feedback process that will allow the system to develop different relational patterns and thereby diminish the need for symptomatic behavior. In this case, the client was warned not to change too quickly because of the potential negative impact on her husband and mother. Her symptomatic behavior was positively connotated and re-framed, indicating strength and protectiveness in relationship to other fam-ily members rather than as occurring out of some internally perceived weak-ness. This connotation touches many different levels of meaning within the client system.

Considering the client's behavior in a simple feedback process (i.e., the client's anxiety increases when she leaves the house and stays stable when she is in the home) is only a partial description of the patterns of interactions. This view describes a simple cybernetic feedback loop analogous to the ther-mostat control process. It fails to consider that the therapist is in the loop and the client's behavior is within the larger system. The therapist is both the observer of the simple cybernetic loop and a part of a higher order feedback loop composed of the therapist, the client, and client's family system. Con-tinuing the thermostat analogy, the individual who adjusts the thermostat is necessarily included in the oscillating loop of ongoing change in order to main-tain temperature stability. He or she is simultaneously the observer and part of the observed, as is the therapist both an observer and a participant in the therapeutic process. All description within a cybernetic system becomes self-referential. What the observer describes is his or her *relationship* to that which is observed.

It is here that a misconception of Ericksonian work often occurs. Many therapists using Ericksonian techniques appear to act as if they can intervene in the client's system from outside the system, that somehow they are objec-tive observers of the therapeutic process. In this view, the therapist simply reorganizes the structure of the family by conscious intention (i.e., prescribes the symptom, gives a task to disrupt the problematic behavior, gives a direc-tive on a better way to interact, etc.). Watzlawick, Beavin, and Jackson (1967) and Haley (1967, 1983) are major proponents of this simple cybernetic pro-cess (Mackinnon, 1983). While these authors have made significant contribu-tions to the technique of therapeutic interventions, inherent in their approach is the view that the therapist intervenes from outside the client system and causes change to occur. The therapist does not cause change to occur. He or she can only provide an opportunity for the client to compensate for the therapist's behavior (therapeutic interventions) which may result in therapeutic change for the client. This argument is not simply one of semantics.

Maturana (1980) referred to the belief in causality as "instructive interac-tion," which implies input "A" results in a specific response "B." This does not seem to be the case in complex human system interactions, simply because the same input rarely, if ever, results in exactly the same output. Erickson would often tell the same story to different clients, who would show different responses. The client responds with his or her own meaning to the therapist's behavior. Maturana contends that one cannot *put* information into a system. The system determines its own response based on its structure. For example, sound waves vibrating at a particular frequency will shatter crystal only because of the structure of the crystal. The crystal has to be at the correct thickness in relation to the sound wave. In the therapeutic context, a client will respond to a therapist's behavior in accordance with his or her structure (i.e., beliefs, world view, personal history, ethnicity, etc.). The therapist can "perturb" the client system in a way to which the client may or may not respond. Telling a metaphor in English to a non-English-speaking client is unlikely to have the desired therapeutic effect. However, telling the same story to an English-speaking client may provide the client the opportunity to develop new meanings, associations, and behaviors based on the client's structure.

A causal view of change implies that the therapist and client are two independently functioning entities and that the therapist acts in a unidirectional manner on the client. The therapist and client, however, form a "whole recursive system" (Keeney, 1983, p. 77) with each influencing the other in a continuous feedback process. Thus, the client intervenes with the therapist by presenting symptomatic behavior to which the therapist responds with his or her own interventions. Each response regulates the response of the other. Given the assumption that all observation is self-referential, then the notion of objectivity (i.e., the separateness of the observed from the observer) is fallacious. Therapists who perceive themselves as separate from their clients, objectively controlling the clients' behavior in a unilateral fashion, trivialize (Von Foerster, 1972) the therapeutic context. A therapist who describes a client in a particular way (e.g., depressed) is not objectively describing the client but is describing his or her *relationship* with that client. A description of relationship as opposed to a description of "reality" creates a different map or context for therapeutic interventions.

A cybernetic view of therapy does not imply that pragmatic interventions should be abandoned. On the contrary, what it does imply is the existence of a higher order of recursion in which the individual is a part of various orders of organization depending on the distinctions or descriptions drawn by the observer. The smallest unit of observation in the therapeutic context, however, is not the individual but rather the client-therapist dyad. Therefore, a cybernetic view implies that specific actions on the part of the therapist occur within a specific context of feedback, not unilaterally from the therapist to the client. For the therapist to ignore the feedback from the client is a mistake that will often lead to no therapeutic change and harm to the client.

This is perhaps a key point from which to consider Ericksonian work. The therapist is simultaneously acting upon and being acted upon in the process of therapy. As Keeney (1983) indicated, if one maintains a cybernetic complementary view, aesthetics and pragmatics, or theory and action, are not mutually exclusive but rather parts of a recursive feedback loop. Aesthetic considerations (patterns of interactions) form a context for pragmatic behaviors (therapeutic interventions) which in turn influence the observation of aesthetic patterns. The individual using Ericksonian techniques needs to be able to make a paradigmatic shift from simple cybernetics (the thermostat analogy) to second-order cybernetics in which he or she is considered part of the process (the observer who is influenced by the temperature to adjust the thermostat), in order to avoid interventions without an aesthetic or theoretical base.

Ericksonian Techniques
Within a Cybernetic Framework

Ericksonian hypnosis differs radically from the standard use of hypnosis in its employment of utilization, indirection, and strategic interventions. Traditional hypnosis relies on the power of the hypnotist to hypnotize the client. He or she induces or "causes" the client to go into a trance. The traditional hypnotist uses suggestions such as "your hand is getting heavier, you will be deeply relaxed, you will go into a deep sleep, etc.," or other direct suggestions aimed at deepening trance and removing the symptom. This view is a linear or causal view of change. However, not all clients respond to such direct suggestions, in which instance the client often is judged (or blamed) not to be hypnotizable (Spiegel, 1972). The recursive process between the client and therapist is missed by the hypnotist in this instance. The language of "hypnotist" and "subject" lends itself to a causal view of hypnosis. Something is done to someone by somebody.

Ericksonian hypnosis is an interactive two-way street. Who is hypnotizing whom is a matter of perspective. From a cybernetic perspective, it is inaccurate to state that the therapist hypnotizes the client or that the client hypnotizes the therapist. Either view is incomplete because both happen simultaneously. Lankton (1983) reported that Erickson often experienced trance when doing hypnotic work. Perhaps a more useful description of the hypnotic interaction is that the hypnotist both hypnotizes and is hypnotized by the client; the same description fits the client in his or her relationship with the therapist. The traditional subject-object perspective (with the client as object) in describing hypnosis is an incomplete description of a larger pattern of interaction. The hypnotic process is a recursive relationship *between* the therapist and client where the behavior of one influences the behavior of the other.

Rossi (Erickson & Rossi, 1979) and Lankton and Lankton (1983) have emphasized three significant areas of Erickson's hypnotic work: (1) the utilization approach; (2) the use of indirection; and (3) the use of strategic interventions, all of which will be considered in a cybernetic model of therapy. Each of these areas speaks to the complementary relationship between stability and change.

Utilization

Utilization involves using and accepting the client's ongoing behavior, perceptions, and attitudes (Haley, 1967; Erickson & Rossi, 1979; Lankton & Lankton, 1983). The client is not asked to conform to the therapist's mode of interaction but rather the client's behavior is accepted and utilized in the treatment process. Haley (1967) provided the dramatic example of the client who could not stop pacing in Erickson's office. Rather than trying to force the man to sit in the chair in order to begin therapy, Erickson asked the man if he was willing to cooperate with him by continuing to pace the floor, to which the man replied that he must continue in order to remain in the office. Erickson had accepted the individual's behavior as a step towards the treatment goal of relaxation and change. In another example, Erickson (Erickson & Rossi, 1979) was ready to begin a hypnotic induction when the individual requested that she smoke a cigarette first. Erickson accepted her request and then began to offer conversational remarks about the feeling of comfort and security in smoking the cigarette. He timed his comments about inhaling and exhaling with her breathing, followed by other suggestions for the client's development of trance behavior.

What has happened here? The clients have presented certain behaviors to Erickson. Erickson accepted the behaviors and he then presented them back to the clients and framed them as necessary for therapeutic progress. The clients accepted Erickson's behavior (the reframing), transformed it (made his or her own unique response), and presented this altered form of the behavior back to Erickson. This interactive process clearly emphasizes the relationship *between* the client and Erickson. Such a transforming or reframing of the client's behavior by Erickson and of Erickson's behavior by the client allowed both Erickson and the client to experience some initial success. This success in turn positively influenced both Erickson and the client and increased expectation of each for change. Here again it is perhaps more theoretically useful to view utilization as a cybernetic process between the client and therapist where each transforms the behavior of the other, forming a new relational pattern between the client and therapist. From this perspective, utilization is far more than a technique that a clever therapist uses to "trick" the client into a desired response.

Indirection

The Ericksonian approach to hypnosis is characterized by the use of indirect suggestions. Rossi (Erickson & Rossi, 1979) categorized approximately 11 indirect suggestions, including truisms, covering all class of possibilities, open-ended suggestions, implication, apposition of opposites, conscious/unconscious dissociation, etc. However, Erickson's use of indirect suggestions has typically been viewed as a technique to overcome the perceived resistance of the client (Haley, 1967; Erickson & Rossi, 1979, 1980; Watzlawick, Weakland, & Fisch, 1974). This view reflects a notion of force and causality as much as the traditional approach to hypnosis and therefore fails to consider the larger therapist-client recursive system. From a cybernetic perspective, the use of indirect suggestions provides a feedback loop between the client and therapist.

Thus, when the hypnotist says, "Perhaps your right hand is getting heavier or lighter or will it remain the same or change in a way that you are not yet certain or will it be your left hand?" the hypnotist has provided maximum opportunity for the client to respond. The therapist has not said what response, if any, the client should make, and has presented information to the client in such a way that any response (no response is a response) is acceptable. As the therapist's suggestions influence the client, so do the client's responses influence the hypnotist's next suggestion.

This is a good example of a cybernetic loop where the performance reorganizes the pattern which regulates the performance. This loop includes the therapist and client in a mutually interdependent relationship rather than the therapist independently causing the client to act in a particular way. The notion of causality is not necessary or useful. This perspective provides an aesthetic basis from which to consider hypnosis and indirect suggestion. The larger inclusive system of client *and* therapist expands the simple cybernetic concept of the thermostat (the client system) to cybernetics of cybernetics (the client-therapist system). The use of specific treatment interventions will be discussed in the following section.

A Recursive Model of Ericksonian Therapy

To separate indirection and utilization from treatment interventions is a purely arbitrary distinction done for discussion purposes. Indirection and utilization are woven through the process of treatment. Prior to a presentation of the recursive relationship between diagnosis, treatment goals, and interventions, a brief discussion of the process of therapeutic change is needed.

Change and Stability

As was discussed earlier, change and stability represent a cybernetic complementarity (Varela, 1976). Each must be considered in the therapeutic process. The old French proverb that states, "the more things change, the more things remain the same" can be inverted to state, "the more things remain the same, the more things change" (Keeney, 1983). The relationship between stability and change is demonstrated in the examples of the tightrope walker who must continually sway in order to remain stable, or the canoer who rocks a canoe in order to maintain its balance.

What changes in a cybernetic system is the relationship of its parts in order to maintain stability of the entire system. For example, a marital couple must continually change in their relationship with each other in order to maintain the stability of the marital system (e.g., one person may show anger while the other experiences depression, and vice versa, or one person may act in a dominant manner while the other acts in a complementary submissive manner). The important point to consider is that any part of one system is only another part in some other higher order system (i.e., the couple's relationship with their own family of origin). Therefore, in order to account for stability in a system, one must consider change in a higher order system; the inverse side is that change in one system is in relationship to the stability of a higher order system. The client in therapy is simultaneously asking for change and stability (i.e., "I want to change this behavior but nothing else" or "fix this child but the family is OK"). The therapist must consider both requests in his response to the client.

A fundamental premise of ecology is that because of the self-corrective oscillating feedback process, the system will eventually heal itself if left alone (Keeney, 1983, p. 162). The therapist's job is to release information or "perturb" the client system so that new relational patterns may form and therefore the system will heal itself. Therapy then becomes the process whereby the system finds its own self-adjustments or aesthetic preference (Bateson, 1972).

Symptomatic behavior by the individual client or within the family is a way for the system to change at one level while remaining stable at a higher order level. Rossi (Erickson & Rossi, 1979) suggested that symptoms may be metaphorical unconscious communication from the nondominant hemisphere about a conflict in a client's life. For Keeney (1983), symptoms are also unconscious communication of a particular epistemological premise, belief, or world view that is ineffective at one level in the system but helps maintain stability at another level in the system. Symptomatic behavior in relationship to the larger system is analogous to the fluctuating thermostat that maintains a steady room temperature.

Therapeutic change for Rossi in describing Erickson's work (Erickson & Rossi, 1979), is typically an unconscious process by which the meaning of the symptom is changed. For example, depression may be reframed as protectiveness of another, or what was viewed as a weakness by the client is redefined as a strength. Tomm (1984), in discussing the Milan approach to change, indicated that therapeutic change is change in a family's map of the world or belief system and typically occurs at the unconscious level. Thus, in the use of positive connotation and circular questioning (Selvini-Palazzoli et al., 1980), the therapist shows the family the pattern that connects them and provides the family the opportunity to reorganize their relational patterns while remaining stable as a family system.

The goal of therapy is to "activate this cybernetic system to provide an alternative higher order feedback correction of the lower order process involving symptomatic escalation" (Keeney, 1983, p. 163). More simply put, the client's symptomatic behavior needs to change at the levels which maintain it. In the case of the client with panic attacks, the relational patterns of the client, her mother, and husband (the higher order system) needed to change before the panic attacks subsided. This process is likely to be most effective when it occurs at the unconscious level because the conscious mind will be unable to make the same associations, connections, or maps that have previously supported the problem. If the therapist fails to consider the larger system of the client and the complementary relationship of change and stability, then he or she may become part of the loop that maintains the symptomatic behavior. Dell (1980) stated that the traditional psychiatric approach to schizophrenia (i.e., identifying the client as "sick," isolation from the family system, hospitalization, etc.) fails to consider the larger systemic interactions and thereby contributes to the very problem it seeks to cure.

How does a client or family change? An important aspect of the process of change and stability is the concept of the random. From randomness new structures can evolve. Bateson (1972) indicated that nothing new can be created in the absence of a source of the random. He cited random mutations in nature as an example of evolutionary development. In Ericksonian therapy, the therapist becomes a source of the random. Of course, the random in therapy is not totally random, but rather information that is potentially meaningful to the client. In responding to the randomness introduced by the therapist, the client will engage in an unconscious search for meaning, and new patterns of behavior can evolve as a result of this unconscious search (Erickson & Rossi, 1980; Lankton & Lankton, 1983).

Milton Erickson was particularly skilled in employing "useful randomness" in the therapeutic situation. His use of confusion, jokes, metaphor, and symptom prescription, to name a few of his interventions, was very effective in disrupting the client's conscious expectations and creating an opportunity for unconscious search and new behavior to emerge (Erickson & Rossi, 1980). Thus, the client presents his or her problem to the therapist who accepts the client's perception. The therapist then transforms the information received by adding a little noise (e.g., a seemingly unrelated story) or disrupts the conscious expectations of the client (with a joke or task) and presents it back in a slightly altered form. The client then transforms it and presents it back in a slightly altered form to the therapist, and so on. Each one's perception and behavior is shaped by the other's in this recursive relationship. The "useful randomness" in this process occurs in the alterations or transformations of the other's behavior such that the therapist and client both search for new meaning in the other's response.

Keeney (1983) provides an insightful example of a cybernetic relationship between Erickson and a client named George. George (cited in Haley, 1967) was a patient in a state hospital for five years. His identity was unknown and he spoke a schizophrenic word-salad. No one was successful in communicating with him. Erickson carefully studied George's speech patterns and learned to speak in a similar style. Thus, when George spoke in an angry word-salad, Erickson spoke in a courteous word-salad. George then answered in a curious word-salad to which Erickson then responded with a courteous word-salad with a different vocabulary.

Erickson constructed a transformation of the client's behavior who in turn constructed a transformation of Erickson's behavior. Erickson's use of a courteous tone indicated a change, while his use of a similar speaking style indicated stability. By using a different vocabulary, meaningful noise or useful randomness was introduced as a way in which an alternative pattern of interaction could be constructed between Erickson and George. George responded to the courteous tone with a curious tone. George eventually spoke in regular English followed by word-salad to which Erickson would respond in English followed by word-salad. In this way a recursive self-correcting relationship was formed between Erickson and George (Keeney, 1983).

Ericksonian use of metaphor is another powerful example of transforming the client's presentation. Through the use of metaphor, the client's presenting problem is accepted and then transformed into a parallel form. Confusion or useful randomness (e.g., as a series of stories) is added in order to disrupt the client's conscious processes and to increase the client's search for new meaning. Suggestions which help the client access needed resources to develop new patterns of behavior are woven into the fabric of the story. During this process, the client is presenting nonverbal responses to the story which are influencing the therapist's telling of the story. Thus, if a client is giving nonverbal signs of agreement or disagreement, the therapist alters his or her story to fit the client's need for stability while material outside the client's conscious mind speaks to the request for change.

Lankton and Lankton (1983) have developed the multiple embedded metaphor technique in which a story is begun and left incomplete, another story is begun and also left incomplete, followed by a third story, and so on, until a story is begun and completed. The stories left incomplete are then finished in the reverse order in which they were stopped. This entire process is confusing and disrupting to the conscious mind of the client as she or he tries to follow all the stories. The stories seek to help the client access the needed resources for therapeutic change within the client's social system. The recursive relationship between the client and the therapist exists in the way the client's problem is transformed through the story and in the way the client transforms the therapist's words for his or her own use and then presents that transformation back to the therapist via perceptual, attitudinal, ideomotor, and/or behavioral changes. In this process, the response of each shapes the response of the other.

Figure 1 presents a recursive model of Ericksonian therapy from a cybernetic perspective.

Client ecosystem. At the top of the figure is the client's ecosystem, that which the client brings into the therapy room. The client comes into therapy with a personal history, world view, role in his or her family, ethnic background, cultural experience, etc. This view emphasizes that the client's behavior is only a part in a larger order recursive system and the client's behavior (symptoms) may be an important aspect in maintaining that stability. The client's symptoms, while a problem at one level in the system, are part of the solution at another level in the system. Within his or her system, the client is continually transforming the information received and presenting it back to the system. However, a symmetrical escalation between the members has occurred such that a recalibration (therapy) is needed in order for the system to maintain itself. If a symmetrical escalation were to continue unchecked, the entire system could break down. The client then enters therapy to prevent further escalation and presents his or her symptomatology to the therapist.

The therapist draws distinctions (diagnostic parameters). Observations about the client are made according to the assumptions and perspectives of the observer. The first act in observing is to draw a distinction (to note a difference that makes a difference). Lankton and Lankton (1983) have proposed six categories of distinctions to be drawn. These categories are referred to as diagnostic parameters. They are: (1) the structure of the social network of the client; (2) the stage of development of the client's family (i.e., career development, retirement, divorce, etc.); (3) the developmental age and task of

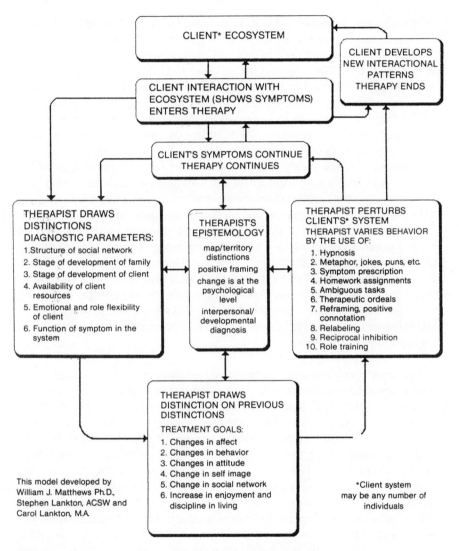

Figure 1. Recursive model of Ericksonian psychotherapy

the client (i.e., infantile, latency, adolescent, college age, married, family, divorced, etc.); (4) the availability of resources of the client; (5) the flexibility and sensitivity of the client in the areas of cognition, perception, behavioral role, and emotion; and (6) the function of the symptom in the system.

   The therapist draws further distinctions (treatment goals). Observations are always made on previous observations. Lankton and Lankton (1983) have identified these distinctions as treatment goals. Goals of treatment are typically associated with the strategic school of therapy (Watzlawick et al., 1967, 1974; Haley, 1967) and are not specifically identified with the systemic approach (i.e., the Milan approach of Selvini-Palazzoli et al., 1980). However, Matthews (1985) has indicated that goals for treatment need not be considered fixed rules for ways in which the client *must* act but rather "perturbations" by the therapist of the client system to which the client system may or may not adjust. As discussed above, the structure of the system determines how it will respond to the information presented. Thus, treatment goals are but information to which the client system will respond depending on its structure.

Erickson (Erickson & Rossi, 1979) and Lankton and Lankton (1983) have indicated that the therapist cannot and need not be certain to what the client will respond when the therapist uses metaphor and other indirect approaches. The latter maintained that the client will make the best choice for him- or herself at the given moment. Thus, the therapist's treatment goals are only distinctions drawn by the therapist to which the client will respond and feed back to the therapist. The treatment goals identified are: (1) changes in affect; (2) changes in behavior; (3) changes in attitude; (4) changes in self-image; (5) changes in social network; and (6) enjoyment and discipline in living (Lankton & Lankton, 1983). These goals can be considered themes for the therapist's perturbations.

Therapist's perturbations (interventions). Multiple embedded metaphor can be employed to provide the client the opportunity to access the needed resources to make the desired changes (Lankton & Lankton, 1983; Matthews & Dardeck, 1985). In addition to multiple embedded metaphor, there is a wide range of therapeutic responses that the therapist can make in transforming and feeding back the response to the client. Figure 1 presents responses (perturbations) such as metaphor, symptom prescription, confusion techniques, homework, irrelevant tasks, ordeals, etc. Each of these responses ought not be considered an intervention to change the client but a response by the therapist to the client's previous response. These therapist behaviors may or may not change the relational pattern between the client and therapist or between the client and his or her ecosystem. While the therapist cannot change the client, the therapist can vary his or her own behavior to increase the probability of a meaningful interaction with the client. Stephen Lankton (1983), in discussing the following clinical case of Carol Lankton, presented a clear example of the cybernetic relationship between the client and the therapist in her use of "ambiguous function assignments."

A client who felt particularly unable to appreciate herself as having value had come to see Lankton. After a number of unsuccessful attempts to reframe the client's experience of herself, Lankton instructed her to carry a 10-pound weight once around the neighborhood and to then state why she was asked to do this task. She returned after her first trip and stated that the weight represented the burdens she put on herself. Lankton responded that they both already knew that and she would not have given a task with such an obvious meaning. The client was then asked to do the task again. Each time she returned, regardless of what she said, Lankton told the client that she did not quite grasp the meaning of the task. When the client finally returned angry, tearful, and unwilling to continue the task, Lankton gave her a delicate art object to carry with the instructions to learn the meaning of this new task. The client returned from her walk with a strikingly different understanding of her own value and was then able to proceed with therapy. The two tasks, juxtaposed, helped create an opportunity for a different perception to occur for both the client and Lankton.

Lankton did not have a specific goal in this process. It was not intended as a paradoxical intervention. The client, however, perceived Lankton as having a specific purpose which she had to discover. Lankton's only purpose was to stimulate the client's thinking by rejecting the client's explanation after each trip around the neighborhood and sending her out one more time. In this interaction, both the client and the therapist are in a recursive relationship, each transforming the other's behavior. The disruptive nature of the tasks, in conjunction with their perceived difference, allowed both Lankton and the client to evolve a new relational pattern (that the client had value as a person) and proceed with therapy.

Development of new interactional patterns (termination). As shown in Figure 1, if the client's relational patterns are reorganized within his or her ecosystem such that the presenting problem has diminished, ceased, or somehow changed, then therapy is terminated. If new relational patterns do not occur, then therapy is continued until new patterns develop. However, if change fails to occur, then the pattern of therapy itself may have become incorporated within the client system such that minimal or no client change maintains the stability of the larger system. The therapist, by continuing to work with only the client, may be intervening at the wrong level in the system and thus perpetuating the problem. At this point in therapy, the therapist needs to consider ways in which to vary his or her own behavior such that the homeostatic client-therapist relationship is disrupted. Failure to do so will result in long-term therapy with little or no change or, client dropout.

Finally, within this recursive model of therapy is the therapist's epistemology, beliefs, world view, maps, etc., constantly informing and being informed by the distinctions drawn and the actions taken. The model in Figure 1 necessarily includes both the therapist and the client and is therefore a model of second-order cybernetics.

Conclusion

The intention of this paper was twofold: (1) to present Ericksonian work as having an aesthetic base in conjunction with its pragmatic utility; and (2) to present a recursive model of Ericksonian therapy rather than a model of causal change. The notion of linear causality, while seductive particularly within western culture, is an epistemological error. The therapist cannot cause change in the client but rather can vary his or her behavior in order for the client to develop new relational patterns within the ecosystem. This emphasis is significant because it frees the therapist from the unfulfillable bind of *changing* the client. The therapist has the responsibility for varying his or her own behavior in relation to the client. The client will respond to the therapist's behavior based on his or her structure, not because the therapist "put information into the client system."

The concept of structural determinism (Maturana, 1980) in which the behavior of the organism is determined by the structure of the organism, not by the external stimulus that might impinge on it, has relevance for the Ericksonian or any therapist. If an organism's behavior were determined by the external stimulus, then its behavior would be absolutely predictable. Therapy would be quite simple and short. Tell the client the way to behave, live, etc. and therapy would be over. Clients rarely, if ever, act in such a straightforward manner. Maturana, a biologist, argues that the organism's behavior is determined by its own structure (i.e., what it is capable of doing). Thus, different clients will respond differently to the same metaphor or therapist behavior. The client will determine how he or she will respond to the therapist's behavior, not the therapist. New relational patterns occur as the result of "structural coupling," where the behaviors of each individual are compensated for by the other's. When the therapist and client are in strong rapport and working well together, then they can be said to be "structurally coupled." Each, therefore, mutually influences the other and new patterns of behavior evolve for both the client and therapist.

Bateson (1972) discussed the evolution of the horse's hoof *and* the turf together as an example of a coevolutionary process. The hoof did not evolve in the absence of the changing turf nor did the turf evolve in the absence of the changing hoof. They coevolved. The same consideration is applicable to the therapeutic process. In Ericksonian therapy, whether the therapist is using hypnotic trance, telling a metaphor, or prescribing symptoms, the therapist and client form a mutually influencing, coevolving pattern of interaction. The notion of causality is nonsensical from a cybernetic perspective. The view expressed here is an attempt to consider Ericksonian therapy from a larger recursive framework and thereby present its aesthetic complement to the already well-known pragmatic utility.

Finally, many theorists (e.g., Haley, 1963, 1967; Lankton & Lankton, 1983; Erickson & Rossi, 1979, 1980; Watzlawick et al., 1967, 1974) have tried to identify what it was that Milton Erickson did. Each has his own view and each, as well as the present author, is both correct and incomplete. Because all observation is self-referential, there can be no objective identification of Erickson's work, but rather a series of perceptions that change and are modified according to new perceptions. The cybernetic view discussed in this article is another perception that seeks to include the therapist as a part of what he or she observes and to present Ericksonian work as a process that coevolves between the client and therapist. Perhaps the most succinct metaphor to describe the recursiveness of the client-therapist system in Ericksonian therapy lies in M. C. Escher's lithograph (Escher & Locher, 1972) of two hands each simultaneously drawing the other, one hand symbolizing the therapist, the other the client; who is who is a matter of perspective.

References

ALLMAN, L. (1982). The aesthetic preference: Overcoming the pragmatic error. *Family Process, 21*, 43–57.

BATESON, G. (1972). *Steps to an ecology of mind.* New York: Ballantine.

DELL, P. (1980). Researching the family theories of schizophrenia: An exercise in epistemological confusion. *Family Process, 19*, 321–335.

ESCHER, M. C. & LOCHER, J. L. (1972). *The world of M. C. Escher.* New York: Harry Abrams.

ERICKSON, M. & ROSSI, E. (1979). *Hypnotherapy: An exploratory casebook.* New York: Irvington.

HALEY, J. (1963). *Strategies of psychotherapy.* New York: Grune & Stratton.

HALEY, J. (1967). *Advanced techniques of hypnosis and therapy: Selected papers of Milton H. Erickson, M.D.* New York: Grune & Stratton.

HALEY, J. (1978). Ideas which handicap therapists. In M. Berger (Ed.), *Beyond the double bind.* New York: Brunner/Mazel.

HALEY, J. (1983). *Ordeal therapy: An unusual way to change behavior.* San Francisco: Jossey-Bass.

KEENEY, B. (1983). *Aesthetics of change.* New York: Guilford Press.

KEENEY, B. & SPRENKLE, D. (1982). Ecosystemic epistemology: Critical implications for the aesthetics and pragmatics of family therapy. *Family Process, 21*, 1–21.

LANKTON, S. (1983). Workshop on Ericksonian hypnotherapy. Boston, MA.

LANKTON, S. & LANKTON, C. (1983). *The answer within: A clinical framework of Ericksonian hypnotherapy.* New York: Brunner/Mazel.

LAING, R. D. (1972). *Politics of the family.* New York: Ballantine Books.

MACKINNON, L. (1983). Contrasting strategic and Milan therapies. *Family Process, 22*, 435–438.

MATTHEWS, W. J. (1985). Ericksonian and Milan therapy: An intersection between circular questioning and therapeutic metaphor. *Journal of Strategic and Systemic Therapies, 3*, 16–26.

MATTHEWS, W. J. & DARDECK, K. (1985). The use and construction of therapeutic metaphor. *AMHCA Journal, 7*, 11–24.

MATURANA, H. (1980). Autopoiesis: A reproduction, heredity and evolution. In M. Zelny (Ed.), *Autopoiesis, dissipative structures, and spontaneous social orders.* Colorado: Westview Press.

ROSSI, E. (Ed.). (1980). *The collected works of Milton H. Erickson, M.D., Vol. 1.* New York: Irvington.

SELVINI-PALAZZOLI, M., BOSCOLO, L., CECCHIN, G., & PRATA, G. (1980). Hypothesizing-circularity-neutrality: Three guidelines for the conductor of the session. *Family Process, 19*, 3–12.

SPIEGEL, H. (1972). The eye roll test for hypnotic susceptibility. *American Journal of Clinical Hypnosis, 15*, 25–28.

SZASZ, T. (1974). *The myth of mental illness.* New York: Harper & Row.

TOMM, K. (1984). One perspective of the Milan approach: Part I. Overview of development, theory, and practice. *Journal of Marital and Family Therapy, 10*, 113–125.

VARELA, F. (1976). Star cybernetics. *The Coevolution Quarterly*, Fall, 62–67.

VON FOERSTER, H. (1972). The perception of the future and the future of perception. *Instructional Science, 1*, 31–43.

WATZLAWICK, P., BEAVIN, J. & JACKSON, D. (1967). *Pragmatics of human communication.* New York: W. W. Norton.

WATZLAWICK, P., WEAKLAND, J. & FISCH, R. (1974). *Change: The principles of problem formation and problem resolution.* New York: W. W. Norton.

WHITAKER, C. (1976). The hindrance of theory in clinical work. In P. Guerin, (Ed.), *Family therapy: Theory and practice.* New York: Gardner Press.

Elements
of an Ericksonian Approach

Carol H. Lankton, M.A.

The ideas that Dr. Erickson conveyed and the principles that he represented, rather than merely his interventions, constitute the elements of an Ericksonian approach. Concepts examined here define an Ericksonian approach as positive and individualistic, strategic, systems-oriented, hypnotic, valuing action over insight, based on utilizing client behaviors, and emphasizing indirect methods of communication.

Elements of an Ericksonian Approach

Milton Erickson was emphatic about the importance of carefully treating each person as an individual, and not according to preconceived notions based on personality theories and rigid approaches to therapy. An Ericksonian approach, then, must be marked by flexibility toward clients who are appreciated for their uniqueness. There are, however, particular attitudes, techniques, and values that are consistently identified and labeled "Ericksonian" by a wide range of his students. The elements of an Ericksonian approach, as presented here, serve only as a general foundation upon which to build therapeutic relationships and specific interventions.

Positive and Individualistic

Erickson did not create or adhere to a comprehensive theory of personality. However, the beliefs he held about people and problems were so consistently conveyed in his writing and training sessions that they give the impression of an underlying framework that can be used to unite the wide variety of Ericksonian techniques and interventions. These beliefs centered around an expectation that people will make the best choice they have learned how to

Address reprint requests to: Carol H. Lankton, M.A., P.O. Box 958, Gulf Breeze, FL 32561.

make, and that people are constantly learning and storing these learnings, even though they are usually unaware of the process. He regularly taught that the unconscious contains a wealth of resource experiences that are acquired and automatically stored in the process of living. He believed that therapeutic change results from helping clients reorganize and reassociate their natural abilities and experiences so that these resources become available in new ways. He accomplished this by using an impressive array of creative techniques which he invented, selected, or modified for each client, depending on careful observation and assessment of that client as a unique product of a unique personal history.

Strategic

Webster defines "strategic" as involving the devising and employing of plans or strategems toward a goal. It is this broad definition I use here to describe an actively involved, goal-oriented Ericksonian therapist who fully intends to influence the experience of his or her clients.

An Ericksonian approach includes a careful assessment of the individual or system to be treated, but emphasizes establishment of treatment goals rather than diagnostic labels. Erickson was known for noticing and understanding the significance of even the smallest nuances of verbal and, especially, nonverbal behaviors in his clients. That he often made rapid assessments should not discount the importance of careful observation and diagnosis. In fact, Erickson's "rapid assessments" need to be considered in the light of his intensive work over half a century in which he systematically and carefully fine-tuned his skills of observation and diagnosis.

Speed of assessment aside, it is necessary for the therapist to understand what a person needs to accomplish or learn in order to grow, develop normally, and be sufficiently happy so that symptom manufacturing is no longer necessary. Once this is understood, interventions expected to achieve or approximate a particular goal can be designed and delivered. In this regard, an Ericksonian approach is strategic and the therapist is actively responsible for setting goals, planning treatment, and delivering interventions designed to accomplish those goals.

This should not be construed as manipulating the client to live by the therapist's standards since goals are set in accordance with the client's stated (or implied) desires for change. A strategic therapist is aware that it is impossible not to influence the client and carefully considers what type of effect he or she intends to create. The client, in fact, is paying to have his or her experience manipulated or influenced by the therapist. The client, however, is fully credited and responsible for actually accomplishing therapeutic goals, since clients will only change in ways that are meaningful and relevant for them. The strategic therapist has no power to coerce, only an opportunity to co-create therapeutic outcomes that are consistent with the client's values.

Systems-Oriented

Using the definition of strategic therapy just presented, it is clear that many approaches to therapy can be considered strategic, certainly the entire range of Ericksonian approaches. And yet the term "strategic therapy" has, instead, become almost synonymous with homework assignments and paradoxical interventions in families. Many strategic therapists who regularly use these techniques credit Erickson with influencing the development of this systems-oriented therapy but perceive a vast discrepancy between themselves and Ericksonian hypnotherapists. But both approaches are strategic in that the therapist actively sets and works to accomplish specific objectives and both are systems-oriented in that they focus on the presenting problems of an individual as only a fragment of the larger system.

A systems-oriented value was apparent in Erickson's work and personal life. He was quite straightforward about his belief that people were usually happiest in traditional marriages, bearing and rearing children. He worked to get people moving normally through the life and family cycles by identifying how they had not satisfactorily adjusted and helping them retrieve or learn necessary attitudes, perceptions, behaviors, emotions, self-images, etc. so that they could meaningfully connect or reconnect with significant others. He frequently used the larger social network to help clients generate resource experiences and always seemed to be working to help clients find and fit comfortably into their place within that network in an ongoing, unfolding way. This emphasis on generative change, or change geared to the whole person in his or her larger social context, is a feature of Ericksonian approaches that differs significantly from traditional symptom-removal therapies, especially traditional hypnosis. An Ericksonian approach will be strategic and systems-oriented regardless of the particular technique being used or the number of clients actually seen in the therapy session.

Hypnosis

Erickson was probably best known as a hypnotist, but one who made a dramatic departure from traditional hypnosis. He blurred the boundaries between what is and is not "official" hypnosis by pointing out the natural availability and common occurrence of trance and trance phenomena. Though he directed clinical hypnosis in an interactive relationship with clients, he encouraged them to focus awareness on and use their own natural abilities to go into trance and find ways to solve their problems by using those same naturally occurring, "common-everyday" abilities that they already knew. In this way, he turned the power over to clients and educated them about the vast and positive power of their own unconscious resources. Because Erickson's inductions of hypnosis were often naturalistically conversational, clients frequently did not realize they had been in trance.

Erickson stressed that hypnosis *per se* could not cure anything. He described it simply as a modality for exchanging ideas. He used it to stimulate the client's own thinking. In most cases, certainly in the majority of cases involving psychodynamically generated symptoms, he used hypnosis not as a context to simply give direct suggestions for symptom removal, but as a communication tool to mobilize personal abilities and unique, multidimensional solutions.

Dissociation between conscious and unconscious functioning frequently formed the foundation of Erickson's inductions as he emphasized their distinctions. He commented about and usually encouraged the conscious mind to go about its usual activity, dispelling the myth that hypnosis deals with only the unconscious mind. Simultaneously, he presupposed a vast store of unconscious resources as he spoke about and to the client's unconscious self.

Action Rather Than Insight

Whether using hypnosis as a modality or not, emphasis was not usually placed on helping clients achieve insight for their problems. Erickson thought that, when solving problems was involved, the person's conscious mind most frequently was concerned with limiting beliefs, prejudices, and ideas about how change was not possible. He emphasized, however, that the person's conscious mind had to be contended with in some manner in order to gain access to the person's unconscious abilities. It is a hallmark of the Ericksonian approach that the conscious mind is often overloaded, confused, distracted, or otherwise bypassed for much of the therapy. Erickson's clients might leave his office amnesic for the session, feeling good but not sure why, wondering what in the world had happened, or perhaps even angry that he had wasted their time. But regardless of the conscious disposition, they usually found that somehow their normal social interaction stimulated an unusual availability of feelings, abilities, perceptions, attitudes, behaviors, or ideas.

This outcome highlights several aspects of Ericksonian therapy: conscious/unconscious dissociation, reassociation of ideas, a systems orientation, and indirection and utilization. Erickson believed that people have all the resources within themselves that they need to solve their problems. However, in certain contexts they don't seem to be able to get to one or another of those resources, perhaps because they don't believe the resource exists or because the social network doesn't encourage or permit its occurrence in a particular context. The social network organization allows and reinforces certain roles and forbids others. The social roles that a person has learned and is expected to play delimit the communications that are available or acceptable. Communication reinforces the belief system and conscious beliefs delimit unconscious resources. Through distraction of the conscious mind and its limiting beliefs, the person's normal frame of reference is temporarily suspended. This alteration creates a therapeutic receptivity or opportunity to have the person retrieve and experience natural abilities that have been forgotten, taken for granted, or disowned due to social pressures and expectations.

These reclaimed natural abilities are then associated with the typical stimuli in the social network so that when the person rejoins the social network and perceives the original stimuli, new or previously unused options are available. The stimuli don't trigger the person's negative or limiting associations, but instead trigger associations to personal abilities. A reassociation of experiential life has taken place. Because resources are usually retrieved and reassociated using indirect techniques, the client is often unaware how much therapy has accomplished until some time and experience with significant others have provided an opportunity to notice changes.

Another Ericksonian aspect of getting the client into action (with or without insight) involves task assignments. Erickson did not confine therapy to his office. He strategically used the educational, social, professional, and geographical resources in the client's environment as a context or background for having learnings *in vivo*. He sent clients to perform a variety of tasks, including consulting with cosmeticians, taking dance or piano lessons, looking up information at the library and climbing Squaw Peak. Many times the task was designed such that the client had an opportunity to develop some aspect of a needed social role. As Erickson stated to one of his students: "In psychotherapy, you don't change anyone. You simply create the circumstances under which the individuals can respond spontaneously and change themselves" (M. Ritterman, personal communication, Feb. 1985). When, for example, Erickson instructed a lonely and depressed client to cultivate African violets and give them away in a specific manner to members of her church congregation (Zeig, 1980, pp. 285-286), he created a context for her to learn nurturing, friendly behaviors that would provide her an opportunity to discover unexpected responses she could elicit from other people, develop an awareness of the beauty and pleasant things around her, and develop a sensitivity to other people and their needs. She didn't have to understand how she had become depressed or how she stopped being depressed.

Utilization

Erickson was known for joining people in dramatic ways that resulted in immediate rapport and credibility. People were willing to do seemingly bizarre things at Dr. Erickson's suggestion (e.g., urinate on their bedsheets, polish floors at 2:00 A.M., spit water through the teeth onto unsuspecting coworkers, etc.), perhaps, in part, because he had communicated a genuine acceptance of the person and even of his or her symptoms as having a reasonable and positive purpose. He was willing to appreciate and strategically incorporate whatever behavior the client offered.

Paradoxical symptom prescription gained considerable attention as an Ericksonian intervention but still is not well understood, even by many who use it. It is generally known that the purpose of using paradoxical prescriptions is, in fact, to get the person to do something else eventually by means of purposefully engaging in a symptom or behavior pattern that had been considered involuntary. But when and how does the shift occur? How are symptoms (or other problems, personality orientations, etc.) paradoxically prescribed so that the client continues the problem in a new way that carries with it an opportunity to learn new options for behavior and freedom from that which has been prescribed? How is the symptom "utilized" to accomplish freedom from the symptom?

Erickson considered even the most "resistive" behaviors from his clients to be their best effort at cooperating and getting their personal and interpersonal needs met (Erickson & Rossi, 1981, p. 16). With this belief as a foundation, the strategic Ericksonian therapist assesses what the client or client system needs to do or learn in order to develop, obtain gratification, etc. without continuing the symptom. Whether this "something" is a set of specific behaviors, attitudes, and avoided emotion, or a complex interplay of all of these, it must be an implied or inherent aspect of the paradoxical prescription. Rarely is it useful to simply prescribe the symptom without modifying it in some way to create therapeutic leverage. This modification might begin by giving a positive interpretation of the symptom as the person's best option for accomplishing, discovering or protecting something. As I see it, therapeutic leverage is furthered by asking that the person engage in the symptom, problem, or personality orientation, *but* in a particular manner that the therapist suggests. When the client agrees, two things will have been accomplished. One, the routine automatic functioning of the problem will have been disrupted; two, more importantly, an alteration in behavior, perception, cognition, etc. will often have been initiated that becomes a foundation for system-wide therapeutic change.

Still, clients don't usually come to therapy expecting to have prescribed to them the symptom or behavior they're hoping to stop. So no matter how palatable or "Ericksonian" the prescription is, and no matter how much rapport exists before it is given, the paradoxical prescription is still an unconditioned stimulus. As such, the person will not have a ready, automatic response and must search internally for an appropriate response. The person's normal framework with regard to that problem will be temporarily suspended since that framework usually does not include any positive belief about the problem and most certainly has not included any idea that it could be beneficial to voluntarily initiate the problem.

This condition of conscious confusion and internal search for meaning supports a therapeutic receptivity in which the therapist can illustrate and elaborate upon the alterations that were suggested or implied along with or contingent to engaging in the symptom. This elaboration and illustration can be done in a variety of ways, but it is most effective when it stimulates the client's own thinking and ideas.

Indirection

This section focuses on Ericksonian methods of indirection for stimulating clients to discover and create their own solutions in response to the therapist's words. Though Erickson communicated quite directly on occasion, he devoted much time to developing therapeutic indirection as a subtle but powerful set of interventions. He believed that people do have the capacity to do their own thinking and solve their own problems despite limiting conscious beliefs. He noticed that direct suggestions were useful only to the extent that clients knew what they wanted, were congruent about wanting to accomplish it, and had the resources necessary to change available and organized. Clients seeking therapy rarely meet these criteria. Therefore, rather than using direct suggestion, Erickson emphasized that indirect communications facilitate an unconscious search and retrieval of personal learnings and abilities that in turn stimulate clients to solve their problems in uniquely effective ways.

Ericksonian methods of indirection include formal categories of verbal indirect suggestions and binds, metaphor, ambiguous function assignments, and a variety of nonverbal communications. With any of these methods, it is important to remember that they will be therapeutically effective to the extent that they are relevant and in the best interest of the client.

Erickson's formal categories of indirect suggestions and binds have been described and illustrated elsewhere (Erickson & Rossi, 1980a, 1980b; Lankton & Lankton, 1983) but should be mentioned in this discussion as an interconnected aspect of therapeutic metaphor. A series of metaphors designed to illustrate or elaborate particular resource experiences (attitudes, behaviors, emotions, trance phenomena, etc.) is an indirect method for stimulating the listener's thinking in those areas described. Using formal indirect suggestions and binds in conjunction with those metaphors, however, will facilitate an even more personal retrieval of the desired experiences.

Erickson told many stories and told them to a variety of clients. As he said of his treatment for a young, anorectic girl: "My treatment for Barbie was to tell her short stories, metaphors, suspenseful stories, intriguing stories, boring stories. I told her all kinds of stories, little stories" (Zeig, 1980, p. 134). He illustrated (often at great length) the experiences he wanted his clients to retrieve as they fixated their attention upon the dramatic aspects of an unfolding storyline about someone else. Clients were free to create their own meaning from the stimulus offered and even have learnings too painful for the conscious mind to tolerate. After all, it was "only a story." As such, metaphor can be considered an altered framework through which a client is free to entertain novel experiences.

Erickson often followed a paradoxical directive with a series of stories. As previously elaborated (Lankton & Lankton, 1983, 1985), a client will develop a particular receptivity to incoming information at the point in therapy when the normal framework has been disrupted and suspended by an unconditioned stimulus such as a paradoxical prescription. A depressed client who is doing nothing, for example, might be told to go ahead and continue to do nothing (for whatever inherent benefit there may be such as arranging priorities before acting), but to do a better job of it. He or she might be further encouraged to carefully monitor for the presence of any unruly urges to do something and then to use any available energy to suppress those urges, so as not to do anything too soon. But, the therapist could add, there is no reason why the client shouldn't feel comfortable while doing nothing. Then, therapeutic experiences to be elaborated might include how one recognizes urges, how urges grow, how to stop thoughts, how to hold a particular image or goal in mind, how to be comfortable, and how to notice comfort, etc. These are experiences the depressed client can associate to and develop while the normal framework about doing nothing is suspended.

Any of the therapeutic goals illustrated with metaphor will be interpreted differently by each client who filters them through perceptions and experiences unique to his or her personal history. But still, the stories are constructed and delivered (emphasizing and detailing particular experiences with indirect suggestions and binds) based on specific therapy goals. These stories stimulate clients to do a good bit of focused thinking which facilitates retrieval of resource experiences not customarily available or associated to in particular problem contexts.

The strategic therapist formulates goals from which to construct interventions, but the client, responding to the interventions by interpreting personal meaning, ultimately selects and "co-creates" the actual result of the story. The client's ideomotor responses as a story is heard and internally "processed" communicate to the therapist a constant flow of diagnostic information that may confirm, add to, or in some cases contradict the original, always tentative, assessment. Changes in behavior, feelings, etc. after the session continue to communicate diagnostic information about the effectiveness of the story as a device to retrieve desired experiences. Extramural learning by the client also provides diagnostic information about the client's ability to "translate" those experiences in therapy into actions with significant others.

At times, however, expected "translations" do not occur despite ideomotor "confirmation" of diagnosis and relevant goals and effectiveness of interventions (i.e., metaphor and indirect suggestions) to retrieve experiences. In these instances, other forms of indirect stimulation may be indicated. Another category of Ericksonian indirection involves behavioral assignments somewhat similar to the task assignments previously discussed, but distinguished by having the purpose of the assignment remain completely vague and ambiguous to the client. Another feature of these "ambiguous function assignments" is the apparent irrelevance of the task. For example, a client might be instructed to carry a hammer with him everywhere he goes for a week. Erickson was rarely or, perhaps, never explicit about why a client or student was to find the Boojum tree near Squaw Peak or in the local botanical gardens and yet he *seemed* to have some purpose in mind. There is, of course, no "one reason" and no "right" answer. The therapist's purpose is to create a context for the client to discover the answer or *an answer* from within.

Ambiguous function assignments are a unique way to get clients in action, both physically and mentally. Because the purpose of the assignment is intentionally withheld from the client, it becomes an opportunity to do a good bit of thinking. For those clients who have accomplished a lot in the therapy sessions but have not integrated those learnings into action, ambiguous function assignments can provide a necessary catalyst. In other cases, therapists may be puzzled about just what it is that a client needs to resolve or learn in order to grow and develop. An indirect stimulation, in the form of an ambiguous function behavior assignment, allows the therapist to diagnose and understand what is relevant for the client as a result of the client projecting meaning into the assignment and reporting it back to the therapist.

Whether the therapist is puzzled about the client's needs or wants a context to help the client integrate relevant therapy learnings, there will always be the element of surprise and discovery for the therapist as the client reports more understandings, insights, ideas, etc. than the therapist could possibly have anticipated. This is the purpose of such assignments with apparently ambiguous functions.

What I refer to as ambiguous function assignments, then, are sophisticated, indirect methods to promote motivation and information. Subsequent utilization of a client's information and behavior is, of course, necessary. Ambiguous function assignments are consistently effective because they draw upon the natural human quality of curiosity, and desire for meaning.

Integration of Components: A Case Example

A variety of ideas, attitudes, orientations, and techniques have been presented and discussed. Integrating these components by means of a case illustration can, perhaps, clarify their interconnectedness. The strategic and systems orientation form the basis for interventions that utilize the client's behavior with hypnotherapy, metaphor, and ambiguous function assignment. More specifically, treatment for this client can be overviewed in terms of the elements of an Ericksonian approach presented here.

1. *Positive and individualistic:* Though the client presented herself in an extremely self-effacing manner and primarily in terms of a specific symptom (colitis), she was viewed as having far more resources than she recognized and she was carefully observed and questioned to understand how she had uniquely developed her particular symptom and attitudinal orientation.

2. *Strategic:* Following the assessment (conducted over a period of months in both written and face-to-face communication), I listed several goals for the therapy and designed interventions that I expected would facilitate the client's accomplishing those goals.

3. *Systems-oriented:* Though this client was seen individually, careful attention was directed to assessing and utilizing her stage of development within her family of origin and her current family relationships. Interventions were designed in accordance with what she needed to learn or retrieve in order to grow and develop normally within that system.

4. *Hypnotic:* Hypnosis was used as the primary context for delivering the indirect treatment interventions of metaphor and indirect suggestion. Conscious/unconscious dissociation allowed and encouraged the client to listen and learn in two modes simultaneously.

5. *Action-vs. insight-oriented:* This client demonstrated considerable insight as to how her problems had developed, but seemed unable to alter her activities and patterns of symptomatic behavior. Therefore, no attempt was made to further insight, but instead indirect methods (metaphor, indirect suggestion, and an ambiguous function assignment) were used to retrieve needed resources (attitudes, abilities, feelings, etc.) that could be directed toward creating new adjustments to current life demands.

6. *Utilization:* Though I held a positive belief about this client that differed significantly from her own personal evaluation, I planned to first utilize her opinions and typical interpersonal orientation (submissive, passively rebellious, self-effacing) to meet her at her familiar model of the world. I paradoxically instructed her to go into trance doubting and criticizing herself and rebelling against my suggestions, so as to validate the genuineness of her experience. This "paradoxical personality orientation prescription" utilized the client's presenting behaviors. The ambiguous function assignment at the

end of the therapy utilized her behaviors of continually looking to the therapist for approval and the "right" answers to her problems. Between these two extremes, verbal and minute ideomotor behaviors were incorporated and utilized in refining diagnostic assessment and fine-tuning selected interventions to "speak to the client's condition."

7. *Indirection:* Finally, as already summarized here, formal categories of indirect suggestion and binds were used in conjunction with metaphor to induce trance and address therapeutic goals. These interventions were followed by the ambiguous function assignment as an indirect stimulus to further crystalize her own interpretations and solutions.

Case Study:
"Getting Real Mileage from Therapy"

In this case, the client, "Mary," a 40-year-old woman, was seen for three two-hour hypnotherapy sessions in a three-day period.* An ambiguous function assignment was given immediately prior to the third and last hypnotic session. Thus, she was given an opportunity to build upon her associations from the previous sessions and simultaneously create a learning set (both physically and psychologically) for her last trance. The assignment was that she walk around the half-mile block outside the office, carrying one or two 14-pound weights until she could tell me why she had been assigned this particular task in this situation. Prior to her arrival that day, she had been instructed to wear comfortable clothes and walking shoes, and to "be prepared to change." Upon arrival, she was told that since this was to be her last session, it should be one that she would remember. She was then given the weights and asked whether she would prefer to carry one or both. Her response to this and the therapeutic utilization of it will be described after a brief summary of her presenting problem and therapeutic goals of her first two sessions.

Mary had presented an array of personal problems and demonstrated somewhat unrealistic expectations of the therapy which would be necessarily brief due to the geographical distance between us. She was from another country and was only visiting in the United States to be present for her father's death. Mary's most specific problem was chronic colitis and related pain; it was significant that her father died of cancer in his colon. Mary's other problems included obsessive eating, depression, obsessive self-effacement, and a

---

*This set of sessions was conducted in Spring, 1984. The treatment interventions were designed in consultation with Stephen R. Lankton.

preoccupation with "limitations" that she firmly believed had been caused by her unfortunate past, particularly a minor sexual trauma at age 11 which had been too frightening to tell her parents. She approached the therapy as a needy, clinging child, torn between her desire to be taken care of and her attitude that she didn't deserve nurturing, either from herself or others. She peripherally discussed concerns about her adequacy as a mother of two teenage children and indicated that she was considering divorce as an escape from an unfulfilling marriage.

Goals for the first two sessions had been to: 1) help her disidentify with her father and his illness, make her peace with him, and say goodbye; 2) help her assist that 11-year-old "part" of herself make a more appropriate transition to womanhood, learning to be comfortable with her sexuality; 3) help her dissolve the barrier she had created and open communication lines with her internalized parent interjects; 4) help her expand her internal map of options to include self-nurturing attitudes and behaviors; 5) disorganize the occurrence of her colitis symptom so that her awareness of any aspect of it would help her associate to incompatible experiences of comfort and relaxation; 6) help her develop attitudes to support giving up her bitterness about the past and create the future she desired with her current family; and finally 7) help her modify her self-image to reflect desired characteristics and incorporate her understanding of herself as changed in accordance with the preceding goals. Specifically, she was to build visual scenarios in which she was interacting in a way she valued with her husband, children, parents, colleagues, etc. Work on all of these goals was directed in the modality of multiple embedded metaphors (Lankton & Lankton, 1983).

Mary's ideomotor responses during the first two trances indicated that she was making appropriate personal applications. She oriented from both trances with amnesia for much of the work and therefore had little conscious understanding about how she had changed. In fact, Mary was quite concerned that she had not changed and pleaded that she be seen for numerous additional sessions. At her last session, she presented a long list of goals for the therapy, all of which had been quite thoroughly addressed in the previous sessions. She had been forewarned that changes initiated in hypnotherapeutic work with her would most likely not be fully apparent to her until after she had returned to her social network and allowed some time to pass.

Mary's clinging dependency and extreme distress that therapy was to end after the third session was an indication to consider using an ambiguous function assignment to facilitate a shift in her energy and frame of reference. Therapeutic goals for the third session were to emphasize self-discipline: growing up, taking responsibility for creating her desired present and future, giving up excuses, etc. As a result of the intensity of her ideomotor responses in the previous work, it was reasonable to expect that she had the resource experiences she would need to actively discipline (and nurture) herself instead of desperately depending on other sources, most specifically a therapist! She was not to indulge in the luxury of passively sitting in trance and receiving from me until she had developed a new expectancy for actively creating, not just waiting to "find" the benefits of her therapy. Thus the prescription was given: "Walk around the block carrying these weights until you can tell me why I sent you. Do you think you'll discover the reason more quickly carrying one or both?"

Mary walked around the block four times, carrying one weight the first time, both weights the second time, just one weight the third time, and a fine crystal vase containing delicate sand dollars the last time. In all, she walked two miles. After each round, she stopped in to present a "reason" for having been given this task. These reasons involved ideas about how she could do things for herself, how carrying weights limited her but increased her endurance, how she should decide to simply abandon her imagined limitations, etc. They became increasingly excellent but each one was met with the reality that though her reason was good, it wasn't the one I had in mind and she was to go again. In actuality, she verbalized some part of the desired understanding and attitude each time and the more rounds she completed the more she improved on her expectancy. It would have been a shame to deprive her of that improvement so she kept going.

After the second round, she was even able to angrily challenge why she should have to come up with the therapist's reason. Why wasn't her own reason good enough? She was complimented for her perceptiveness and encouraged to ponder about the answer to her own question. At the end of the third round, the weight was exchanged for the glass vase with the instruction that she would certainly learn something different that time which would finally prepare her for the hypnosis portion of her session. Certainly, any of her previous explanations based on burden and suffering were no longer applicable or were cast in greater doubt than before.

When Mary returned from the last walk, she entered the office tearfully and quietly, and sat down. Demonstrating a range of emotion, she reported that she had been touched to realize that I would trust her to carry something so delicate and fragile and that she had lived up to that trust by carrying it carefully. She emphasized her understanding that the fragile vase was not unlike that delicate and valuable part of herself that she had been entrusted to carry. Then, with tears beginning to stream down her face, she admitted that at one point she had experienced a strong urge to throw down and destroy the vase in anger, much as she was often tempted to end her life rather than be responsible for it. At this point of self-awareness, tender emotion, and physiological confusion, she was asked to go into trance.

For the next hour, a series of metaphors dealing with motivation, sincerity, responsibility, self-discipline, and challenge were presented. Some of these were borrowed from Dr. Erickson's work, such as a recounting of the 50-year-old woman who approached him hoping to use hypnosis to stop smoking. His response to her was that in his experience, women in her age group who wanted to use hypnosis to stop smoking usually weren't sincere and so in order for her to prove her sincerity, he wanted her to climb Squaw Peak each morning at sunrise for one week and see him only after she had done so (Erickson, 1979). Since this ambiguous behavior prescription was quite similar to the one Mary had just enacted, it was certain to capture her interest with the possibility that the "real" reason for her prescription would finally be revealed. Though each metaphor hinted at some such reason, this was never explicitly stated. Thus, in the trance, my reason (which was actually for her to create her own understanding and meaning) was not imposed on her but she was stimulated to elaborate her understanding of her own reasons and personal meaning.

In the process of saying goodbye, Mary was encouraged to create situations for herself that would feel unfamiliar and possibly uncomfortable so as to stimulate her discovering the changes she had begun in the therapy. She left with a peaceful feeling of completion and commented about how the behavior prescription had been an exciting experience for her. Without that prescription as a catalyst to motivate her active participation in making and meeting therapy goals, it is likely that she would have left therapy reluctantly and with a sense of being incomplete. Instead, she is still constructing personal understandings from her own ideas she initiated during those longest miles. She no longer considers suicide and she is now reporting a happy adjustment in her marriage.

Conclusion

This paper has emphasized a number of aspects and elements inherent to an Ericksonian approach, with the understanding that there is no single, identifying manifestation of an Ericksonian approach. There are only ideas and values that Erickson seemed to hold and a variety of interventions that he developed or popularized in his quest to understand and assist unique individuals, utilizing whatever behavior or problems they presented. There was never one right way, just as there is no one approach. Each practitioner will modify these ideas and this information in accordance with personal values and stylistic orientations, just as every student or client who climbed Squaw Peak came down with a unique interpretation of the assignment and "intended" understandings. Perhaps this is what Erickson truly intended in the legacy he left to students of his approach.

References

ERICKSON, M. H. (1979). Taped seminar. The Milton H. Erickson Foundation, Phoenix, AZ.

ERICKSON, M. H. & ROSSI, E. L. (1980a). Variety of double binds. In E. L. Rossi (Ed.), *The collected papers of Milton H. Erickson on hypnosis: Vol. 1. The nature of hypnosis and suggestion* (pp. 412–429). New York: Irvington.

ERICKSON, M. H. & ROSSI, E. L. (1980b). The indirect forms of suggestion. In E. L. Rossi (Ed.), *The collected papers of Milton H. Erickson on hypnosis: Vol. 1. The nature of hypnosis and suggestion* (pp. 452–477). New York: Irvington.

ERICKSON, M. H. & ROSSI, E. L. (1981). *Experiencing hypnosis: Therapeutic approaches to altered states*. New York: Irvington.

LANKTON, S. & LANKTON, C. (1983). *The answer within: A clinical framework of Ericksonian hypnotherapy*. New York: Brunner/Mazel.

LANKTON, S. & LANKTON, C. (1985). Ericksonian styles of paradoxical therapy. In G. Weeks (Ed.), *Promoting change through paradoxical therapy*. Homewood, IL: Dow Jones-Irwin.

ZEIG, J. (Ed.). (1980). *A teaching seminar with Milton H. Erickson*. New York: Brunner/Mazel.

Hypnotic Suggestion for the Control of Bleeding in the Angiography Suite

William O. Bank, M.D.

Control of bleeding with hypnotic suggestions, even in hemophiliacs, has been well documented (Dubin & Shapiro, 1974; Lucas, Carroll et al., 1962; Lucas, Finkelmann & Tocantins, 1962; Thompson, 1969; Kroger & DeLee, 1957; August, 1965; Clawson & Swade, 1975). Medical hypnosis has been applied to neuroangiographic procedures, mostly for the control of pain and anxiety (Bank & Kerber, 1979; Bank & Newfield, 1981). During a 22-month period we have used hypnotic suggestions to control the occasional oozing of blood which occurs *around the angiographic catheter* during the procedure and *at the puncture site* following catheter removal. We recently used similar suggestions in the angiographic suite on a patient with an acute gastrointestinal hemorrhage with apparent success. Our experience with hypnosis for the control of bleeding will be discussed with quotation of typical suggestions used, stressing their brevity.

Introduction

For many years clinical hypnosis has been used successfully in medicine and dentistry. Not only can profound anesthesia be achieved (Esdaille, 1850; Masson, 1955; Crasilneck, McCranie & Jenkins, 1956; Crasilneck, Stirman et al., 1955; Marmer, 1956, 1959), but autonomically controlled functions such as salivation (Dubin & Shapiro, 1974; Miller, 1969), blood pressure (Deabler, Fidel et al., 1973), heart rate (Bleecker & Engel, 1973), skin temperature (i.e., blood flow) (Roberts, Kewman & MacDonald, 1973; Jacbon-

Address reprint requests to: William O. Bank, M.D., C.M.I., 15233 Ventura Blvd. West Plaza, Sherman Oaks, CA 94103.

son, Hacket et al., 1973), and bleeding (Dubin & Shapiro, 1974; Lucas, Carroll et al., 1962; Lucas, Finkelmann et al., 1962; Thompson, 1969; Kroger & DeLee, 1957; August, 1965; Clawson & Swade, 1975) can be modified.

We have used medical hypnosis to relieve anxiety and to provide analgesia during angiography* and embolization** in the cervicocephalic region (Bank & Kerber, 1979). During and following extensive embolization in the territory of the external carotid artery, hypnotic suggestion obviated the need for analgesics or narcotics (Bank & Kerber, 1979). While formal induction of trance was performed on the patients in that initial study, we have found it to be superfluous in most cases and we now use informal techniques of suggestion in our angiography suite (Bank & Newfield, 1981). Less than 1 percent of our patients require medication before or during angiograms, even if they are having large volume peripheral run-off studies.†

Reports of successful hypnotic control of bleeding in hemophiliacs undergoing oral surgical procedures (Dubin & Shapiro, 1974; Lucas, Carroll et al., 1962; Lucas, Finkelmann et al., 1962) encouraged us to use suggestion in patients who oozed blood around the entry site of angiographic catheters and in patients for whom postangiographic hemostasis was difficult to achieve.

Methods and Results

Control of Pericatheter Bleeding

The late Milton H. Erickson, M.D. demonstrated the efficacy of confusion and stress for rapid induction of profound degrees of trance (Erickson, Rossi & Rossi, 1976; Zeig, 1980). Following these concepts, the normal confusion and stress experienced by a patient at the beginning of an angiogram are accepted as adequate "trance induction" and the patient is addressed as if he were obviously in trance (Cheek, 1962). The suggestions that we use to encourage patients to stop bleeding when oozing around the catheters occurs are as simple as the following (which was recorded and transcribed verbatim):

*X-ray studies of the blood vessels which require the injection of an x-ray contrast medium (or dye) into the arteries or veins. The dye produces a sudden warm or burning sensation in the region being studied.

**Intentional injection of vessel occluders into arteries feeding an abnormality. This evokes ischemic pain in the territory which has been deprived of its blood supply.

†Greater than 90% of the patients who undergo angiograms in this country are premedicated with a combination of intramuscular narcotics and sedation (e.g., Demerol 50–75 mg IM plus Seconal 75–100 mg IM) or oral diazepam 10 mg.

"Excuse me, Mr. . . . , but you are leaking a little blood around the catheter where it goes into the artery, and it really does make things a little more difficult for us. If you would just *stop the bleeding*, it would be a big help."

It is surprising how many patients accept this suggestion with no further comment necessary (Cheek, 1962). If their response is an incredulous gaze or a question as to "How?", the patient's confusion is accepted and utilized with the following additional verbalization:

Knowing "how" doesn't really matter, as long as you let it happen. If you think about it, you really have been controlling your bleeding all your life, allowing it to stop when you get cut or scratched *without conscious effort*. I imagine it's similar to the way you speed up or slow down your heart rate, raise or lower your blood pressure, or many of the other things you do *unconsciously*. You don't have to worry about success because we can still get the study done, but if you would just *let it stop*, then things would go along much more easily.

It should be emphasized that these suggestions are given in a matter-of-fact manner by the physician, displaying great confidence that the patient will succeed. This provides a nonverbal reinforcement of the basic suggestion. The exact wording is adapted to the individual patient as necessary, but even the "cookbook" approach with verbatim quotation of a verbalization (such as the above) will usually provide the same results, even when given by an agnostic resident.

Before we started using these suggestions, we would control this kind of bleeding by placing a sandbag wrapped in sterile towels over the catheter's skin-entry-point during time when catheter manipulation was not necessary. This problem occurred about once per month (4 percent of our cases). Since we have been using these suggestions, 24 patients have stopped oozing blood around catheters following suggestions during the past 22 months; the sandbag has been used but twice.

Hemostasis Following Catheter Removal

Similar suggestions to stop bleeding are routinely given at the time of catheter removal and only three patients out of 300 required pressure for more than 10 minutes. One patient with normal clotting studies bled after his arterial puncture site had been held for 10 minutes. His artery was held for an additional 10 minutes but continued to leak when released. When asked if he would please stop bleeding, he replied, "No." When asked why, he responded, "Because you haven't brought me the urinal." He was asked if that was the *only* reason he would not stop bleeding, and when he said yes, he was told "it seemed like a reasonable *condition*." The urinal was provided and the artery released with the comment: "Now that you have the urinal, you can stop bleeding." No further bleeding occurred.

Since all bleeding stops (. . . eventually), it is impossible to quantify the contribution of these simple suggestions to the hemostasis eventually achieved, but the suggestions are easy to give and have no adverse effects. If one considers the requirements of the dentist, plastic surgeon, or general surgeon, and the degree of analgesia and control of physiologic parameters which are requisite to the procedures they have been able to accomplish solely with medical hypnosis, and if one then compares this to the needs of the radiologist performing angiography and special procedures (i.e., relief of anxiety, mild analgesia, sedation, immobility, and cooperation), one wonders why hypnosis has not been employed more frequently as an adjunctive technique in the radiology department.

Unusual Applications of Suggestion

Our experience with the use of suggestion in the relatively routine instances just described, as well as our knowledge of more dramatic accomplishments in cases of hemophiliacs with antibodies to factor VIII and cases of acute trauma with major hemorrhage, led us to use hypnosis in the following case.

Case Report

A 33-year-old veteran had undergone a left radical neck dissection in May 1975 for a malignant tumor (amelanotic melanoma) of the left cheek. He did well until April 1980 when he developed dull pain without radiation, nausea, vomiting or diarrhea. The pain was most severe after eating and was unrelieved by medications.

His pain and an 11-pound weight loss in a one-month period led to reevaluation. Upper GI series revealed a 3 x 3cm mass in the second portion of the duodenum. Chest films showed both hilar and mediastinal adenopathy. Mediastinoscopy with biopsy revealed only "reactive hyperplasia" of the nodes without evidence of tumor. Duodenoscopy with biopsy produced highly anaplastic tumor consistent with amelanotic malignant melanoma.

Shortly after his admission to the San Francisco Veterans Administration Medical Center, he developed ascending cholangitis with sepsis and his blood cultures were positive for *Escherichia coli* and *Bacteroides fragilis*. His liver function was deteriorating. Cholecystostomy with T-tube drainage of his common bile duct improved his clinical condition and bypass of his duodenal tumor was considered.

Before this palliative operation could be performed, the patient developed a massive upper GI hemorrhage, losing 12 units of blood in a 6-hour period preceding an emergency (midnight) angiogram. Embolization of the bleeding arteries was requested if the bleeding point could be identified.

The entire verbalization used for the control of this patient's bleeding is quoted to emphasize its brevity. Upon the patient's arrival in the angiography suite, the angiographer introduced himself and said:

> This may seem strange, but has anyone asked you to stop bleeding yet?

The patient's quizzical look and verbal response of "no" elicited the following short verbalization:

> Then why don't you stop bleeding?, *now!* I know it *sounds* like an unusual request, but it really would help us to help you; and after all, you really have been controlling your own bleeding — all of your life — probably without knowing consciously what you have been doing. You get cut or scratched and you *stop bleeding*, just like you increase your heart rate when you get frightened, and you slow it when you relax — you *do it*, but you don't know how. So you don't need to *consciously* know how you stop your bleeding, but it *will* help us if you just *let it happen*, . . . *now!*

The clearly evident confidence of the angiographer in the patient's ability to fulfill this request served as a strong nonverbal reinforcement of the suggestion.

Angiography was then performed. To minimize dilution of the contrast agent in the venous phase, double catheter technique was used to allow simultaneous injection of contrast agent into both the celiac and the superior mesenteric arteries. One hundred ml of Renographin 76 was injected through the two 5 French polyethylene catheters at a combined injection rate of 18 ml/sec. The tumor could be seen in the territory of the gastroduodenal artery (Figs. 1a and 1b), but no extravasation of the contrast medium was identified.

The gastroduodenal artery was then catheterized selectively with one of the 5 French catheters, and 24 ml of Renographin 76 was injected at a rate of 8 ml/sec (Figs. 2a and 2b). Although tumor staining was intense, no pooling of contrast agent served to identify an active bleeding site.

The catheter was left in place and the following suggestion given:

> So far you have really done well. You have stopped your bleeding completely. But in order to show what *was* bleeding, you now need to *undo* whatever it was that you have done. You don't need to know how, but just let it go ahead and bleed, *now*, so we can see if we have found the correct spot.

The selective gastroduodenal angiogram was repeated without further delay.

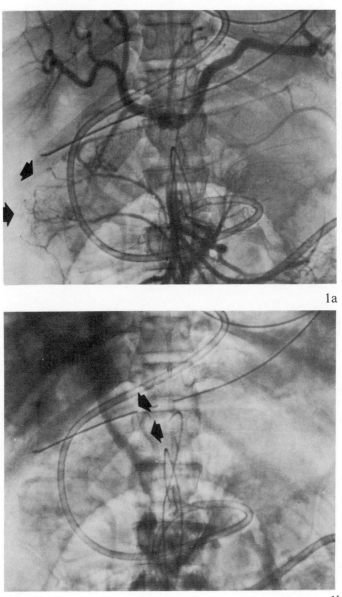

1a

1b

Figure 1. Simultaneous celiac/superior mesenteric angiogram obtained about 30 minutes following the suggestion to stop bleeding. In the arterial phase (Fig. 1a), stretched arteries (arrows) locate the tumor in the duodenum and mesentery. In the venous phase (Fig. 1b), a filling defect in the portal vein (arrows) demonstrates the extensiveness of the tumor, but no pooling of contrast agent defines a bleeding site.

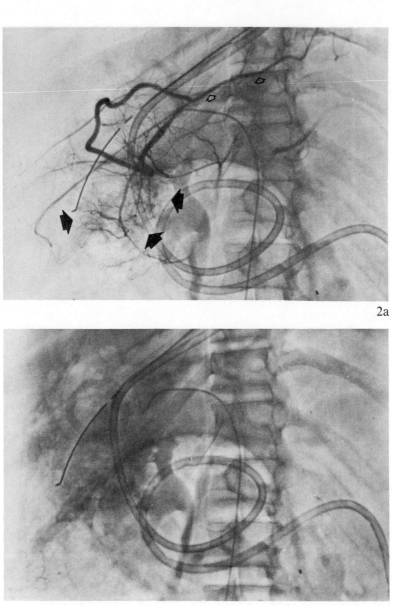

2a

2b

Figure 2. Selective gastroduodenal angiogram, also after the suggestion to stop bleeding. In the arterial phase (Fig. 2a) multiple abnormal arteries mark the location of the tumor (solid arrows). The gastroepiploic artery (open arrows) distal to the tumor will be at risk during particulate embolization. In the venous phase (Fig. 2b) no pooling of contrast agent defines the bleeding site.

It demonstrated rapid extravasation of contrast agent which pooled in the duodenum and antrum of the stomach (Figs. 3a and 3b).

Because of the presence of a large gastroepiploic artery distal to the major blood supply of the tumor (Fig. 2a), and the possibility of ischemic complications in the stomach or bowel, it was elected to postpone therapeutic embolization that night pending more thorough consultation with the several clinical services involved in this patient's care. The suggestion to stop bleeding was repeated and the examination terminated.

The patient had received two additional units of blood during the angiogram. During the ensuing twelve hours he required an additional three units of blood to maintain his hematocrit at 27. In consultation with his family and attending physician it was decided to proceed with the embolization in hopes of achieving palliation sufficient to permit the patient to return home. That afternoon the patient returned to the angiography suite for Gelfoam embolization of the gastroduodenal artery (Fig. 4) and one superior mesenteric branch which was also contributing to the tumor. Bleeding was controlled by this procedure and no subsequent bleeding occurred for 4 days.

On the evening of the fourth day postembolization the patient began bleeding again and passed necrotic tumor per rectum. Exploratory laparotomy and gastrojejunostomy, performed to relieve his bowel obstruction, demonstrated multiple metastatic deposits in his small intestine. Postoperatively the patient continued to bleed and died of cardiac arrest.

At necropsy the duodenal tumor was a 5×5 cm nodule of an $18 \times 10 \times 5$ cm mass in the adjacent mesentery. Other tumor metastases were present in the jejunum, chest and mediastinum as well as in the left neck.

Discussion

Modern investigation of the potential clinical uses of hypnosis was stimulated by observations made during World War II (Beecher, 1946; Sampimon & Woodruff, 1946). Since that time hypnosis has been used successfully both in conjunction with more traditional methods of anesthesia (Crasilneck, Stirman et al., 1955), and as the *sole* means of anesthesia in patients with contraindications to these conventional techniques (Masson, 1955; Sampimon & Woodruff, 1946; Weyandt, 1976).

Aside from its more accepted use as an anesthetic, hypnosis has been used to control bleeding in surgical procedures ranging from cesarean section to rhinoplasty and dermabrasion (Thompson, 1969; Kroger & DeLee, 1957; Marmer, 1956). The absence of swelling and ecchymosis of the eyelids following rhinoplasty is a definite advantage to the use of hypnosis, but it is nowhere near as striking as the missing mist of blood during dermabrasion as documented in Thompson's movie (Thompson, 1969).

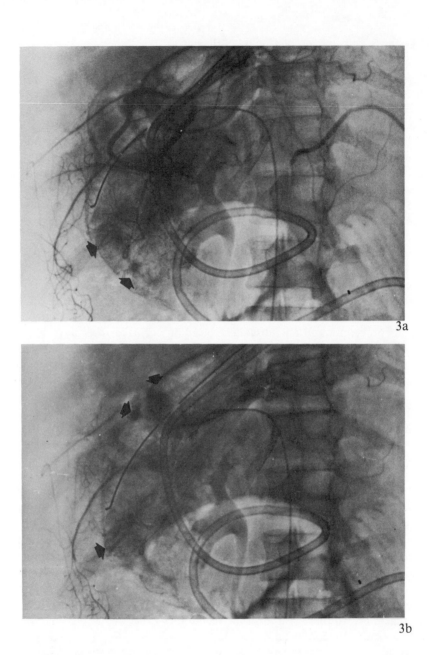

3a

3b

Figure 3. Repeated gastroduodenal angiogram obtained within 10–15 minutes of the first (Fig. 2), but only 1 minute after a new suggestion to "Let it bleed." Tumor staining is more dense in the arterial phase (Fig. 3a) and pooled contrast agent (Figs. 3a & 3b, arrows) can be seen within the duodenum in both the arterial phase (Fig. 3a, arrows) and the venous phase (Fig. 3b, arrows).

84

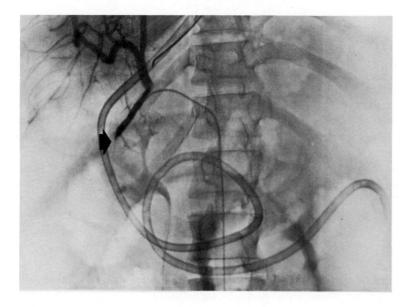

Figure 4. Selective gastroduodenal angiogram after embolization with particulate Gelfoam. The arrow marks the point of occlusion. Note the patency of the common hepatic artery.

Dentists have used hypnosis not only to alleviate pain and anxiety but also to control salivation, swelling, and bleeding both during and following dental extractions in hemophiliacs with contraindications to the use of factor VIII (Dubin & Shapiro, 1974; Lucas, Carroll et al., 1962; Lucas, Finkelmann et al., 1962). Knowledge of these works and our experience with hypnotic techniques led to our use of suggestion in the patient we have reported here. The entire verbalizations used in this case have been presented to stress their brevity.

How can a patient stop bleeding from a tumor that really should not respond to normal physiologic controls? Does he produce spasm in normal feeding arteries? . . . activate clotting factors? Neither hemophiliacs nor the physicians who work with them have a logical explanation of *how* they achieve their dramatic results without demonstrable circulating factor VIII; we can do no better.

Did our patient really respond to the sequence of suggestions given, or was it mere coincidence? We know empirically that he was bleeding profusely before the angiogram and during the final series, but he was not bleeding significantly during the first two angiographic series nor during the interval between the angiogram and the embolization the next afternoon. Though it is clearly difficult to obtain strict scientific data to confirm a causal relationship in this type of situation, it is our strong impression that the sequence of suggestions was effective in assisting the patient to achieve control of his bleeding.

In like manner, although we have demonstrably fewer problems with peri-catheter oozing of blood during angiograms and hemostasis following catheter removal, causal relationship can be disputed by the agnostic on the basis of frequent coincidence. Yet once skeptical residents who were required to give "cookbook" suggestions were so impressed with their effectiveness that they continue to use these suggestions now that their residencies are finished.

In all cases, and most notably the one reported in detail, the important fact is that the use of these suggestions required neither additional time nor extra effort, since they were given by the angiographer while he gowned and gloved. There was no cost for additional medications, nor were there fees for additional physicians. If the suggestions were totally ineffective, nothing was lost. If, on the other hand, the patient's responses were related to the sequence of suggestions, then they helped stabilize his condition at a critical moment, allowing his physicians time for thoughtful decision-making in regard to his therapy.

Conclusion

Training in the use of medical hypnosis develops an acute awareness for the power incorporated in the words we use when talking to our patients, as well as the possibility of simultaneous but entirely different meanings reaching different levels of the patient's conscious/subconscious mind. Knowledge of the physiologic effects achieved by others allows us to convincingly ask our patients to do likewise, knowing that if they fail we have lost nothing, while if they succeed we have made our work easier and allowed our patients to be more comfortable by means of a few well-chosen words.

Author's Note

Although it is possible to read about and then successfully utilize some of the techniques described here or in the references cited, we would like to caution the reader about this "cookbook" approach to hypnosis. Initial experience is most effective if gained under supervision of experienced medical practitioners. This kind of training is available through the Continuing Education Departments of several medical schools and also at workshops sponsored by the Milton H. Erickson Foundation, 3606 North 24th Street, Phoenix, AZ 85016, and by the American Society of Clinical Hypnosis, 2400 East Devon Avenue, Suite 218, Des Plaines, Illinois 60018.

Acknowledgments

I wish to express my indebtedness to Kay Thompson, D.D.S., who introduced me to the late Milton Erickson, M.D. This work is the result of their inspiration and encouragement to me for my application of techniques of medical hypnosis to the practice of radiology. I must also thank Charles W. Kerber, M.D. and Orlow Clark, M.D. for their critical reviews of this paper.

References

AUGUST, R. (1965). *Hypnosis as sole anesthesia for caesarian section.* Kalamazoo MI: Upjohn Film #19.

BANK, W. O. & KERBER, C. W. (1979). Medical hypnosis during therapeutic embolizations of the carotid and vertebral arteries. *Neuroradiology, 17,* 249-252.

BANK, W. O. & NEWFIELD, P. M. (1981). Anesthetic considerations for radiologic procedures. In A. Margulis & C. Gooding (Eds.), *Diagnostic radiology* (pp. 159-168). San Francisco: University of California Printing Department.

BEECHER, H. K. (1946). Pain in men wounded in battle. *Annals of Surgery, 123,* 96-105.

BLEECKER, E. R. & ENGEL, B. T. (1973). Learned control of cardiac rate and cardiac conduction in the Wolff-Parkingson-White syndrome. *New England Journal of Medicine, 288,* 560-562.

CHEEK, D. B. (1962). Importance of recognizing that surgical patients behave as though hypnotized. *American Journal of Clinical Hypnosis, 4,* 227-238.

CLAWSON, T. A. & SWADE, R. H. (1975). The hypnotic control of blood flow and pain. *American Journal of Clinical Hypnosis, 17,* 160-169.

CRASILNECK, H. B., McCRANIE, E. J., & JENKINS, M. T. (1956). Special indications for hypnosis as a method of anesthesia. *Journal of the American Medical Association, 162,* 1606-1608.

CRASILNECK, H. B., STIRMAN, J. A., WILSON, B. J., McCRANIE, E. J., & FOGELMAN, M. J. (1955). Use of hypnosis in management of patients with burns. *Journal of the American Medical Association, 158,* 103-106.

DEABLER, H. L., FIDEL, E., DILLENKOFFER, R. L., & ELDER, S. T. (1973). The use of relaxation and hypnosis in lowering high blood pressure. *American Journal of Clinical Hypnosis, 16,* 75-83.

DUBIN, L. J. & SHAPIRO, S. S. (1974). Use of hypnosis to facilitate dental extraction and hemostasis in a classic hemophiliac with high antibody titer to factor VIII. *American Journal of Clinical Hypnosis, 17,* 79-83.

ERICKSON, M. H., ROSSI, E. L., & ROSSI, S. I. (1976). *Hypnotic realities.* New York: Irvington.

ESDAILLE, J. (1850). *Hypnosis in medicine and surgery.* New York: Julian Press. (Republication date: 1957).

JACBONSON, A. M., HACKETT, T. P., SURMAN, O. S., & SILVERBERG, E. L. (1973). Raynaud Phenomenon. Treatment with hypnotic and operant technique. *Journal of the American Medical Association, 225,* 739-740.

KROGER, W. S. & DeLEE, S. T. (1957). Use of hypnoanesthesia for caesarean section and hysterectomy. *Journal of the American Medical Association, 163,* 442-444.

LUCAS, O. N., CARROLL, R. T., FINKELMANN, A., & TOCANTINS, L. M.
(1962). Tooth extraction in hemophilia: Control of bleeding without use of blood,
plasma, or plasma fractions. *Thrombosis et Diathesis Hemorrhagica, 8*, 209–220.
LUCAS, O. N., FINKELMANN, A., & TOCANTINS, L. M. (1962). Management
of tooth extraction in hemophiliacs by the combined use of hypnotic suggestion,
protective splints and packing sockets. *Journal of Oral Surgery, Anesthesia, and
Hospital Dental Service, 20*, 34/488-46/500.
MARMER, M. J. (1956). The role of hypnosis in anesthesiology. *Journal of the Amer-
ican Medical Association, 162*, 441–443.
MARMER, M. J. (1959). Hypnoanalgesia and hypno-anesthesia for cardiac surgery.
Journal of the American Medical Association, 171, 512–517.
MASSON, A. A. (1955). Surgery under hypnosis. *Anesthesia, 10*, 295–299.
MILLER, N. E. (1969). Learning of visceral and glandular responses. *Science, 163*,
443–445.
ROBERTS, A. H., KEWMAN, D. G., & MacDONALD, H. (1973). Voluntary con-
trol of skin temperature: Unilateral changes using hypnosis and feedback. *Jour-
nal of Abnormal Psychology, 82*, 163–168.
SAMPIMON, R. H. L. & WOODRUFF, M. F. A. (1946). Some observations concern-
ing the use of hypnosis as a substitute for anesthesia. *Medical Journal of Australia,
1*, 393–395.
THOMPSON, K. (1969). *Rhinoplasty and dermabrasion under hypnosis*. Pittsburgh,
PA: Motion Picture Film Services, Inc.
WEYANDT, J. A. (1976). Hypnosis in a dental patient with allergies. *American Jour-
nal of Clinical Hypnosis, 19*, 123–125.
ZEIG, J. (1980). *A teaching seminar with Milton Erickson*. New York: Brunner/
Mazel.

Therapeutic Strategies for the Treatment of Depression

Michael D. Yapko, Ph.D.

Patterns of hypnosis and strategic psychotherapy may be effectively used in the treatment of depressed clients. Hypnosis may be used symptomatically or dynamically; hypnotic strategies involving pattern interruption, reframing, metaphors, symptom substitution, age regression, dissociation, and other hypnotic patterns are described. Strategic psychotherapy approaches involving behavioral directives, symptom prescriptions, and homework assignments are also offered as means of addressing the most common dynamics associated with depression. These dynamics include an ambiguous sense of responsibility and control, and faulty attributions of blame. Contraindications for these strategic patterns are also discussed.

In this paper therapeutic strategies are presented that may be utilized in the treatment of depressed individuals. The interventions presented here are focused on resolving some of the more common dysfunctional patterns underlying depressions. These include self-limiting perceptions relating to issues of personal responsibility, blame, and perceived locus of control.

While family therapy can be effectively utilized in the treatment of depression, in many cases such approaches may be impractical. For this reason the patterns in this paper are generally discussed in the context of individual psychotherapy. Strategies involving the formal use of hypnosis are discussed in the section on "Hypnotic Approaches," while strategies using hypnosis informally in conjunction with other directive approaches are described in the section on "Strategic Approaches."

Address reprint requests to: Michael D. Yapko, Ph.D., The Milton H. Erickson Institute of San Diego, 2525 Camino Del Rio South, Suite 225, San Diego, CA 92108.

Hypnotic Approaches

Hypnotic approaches may be used symptomatically or dynamically (Yapko, 1984a). Dynamic approaches, i.e., those that address both the symptom and underlying causes, are generally more intensive and are thus more likely to accomplish a fuller resolution of client problems, but more superficial approaches can be used with some success in the treatment of depression.

Depression, at the intrapersonal level, is an inwardly focused and subjectively uncomfortable experience, and often the client is only painfully aware of what seems to be a useless set of symptoms. Depression is not the inactive state it may superficially seem to be to the casual observer. It is a state of ongoing internal agitation and discomfort, involving anxiety and perseveration of negative feelings and thoughts. Hypnosis aimed at symptom removal can serve as a "pattern interruption" intervention, and can also serve as an opportunity for "reframing" (Erickson & Rossi, 1979).

Nondynamic Approaches

1. Pattern interruption. Pattern interruption through hypnosis may be accomplished simply through attainment of relaxation via the induction and general suggestions for relief. Given the generalized anxiety and negatively skewed cognitive distortions of the depressed condition, even the simplest of inductions and therapeutic suggestions can have a beneficial effect.

The negative patterns are interrupted by facilitating relaxation and focusing the individual on positive possibilities. The implicit messages to the depressed individual are that a change in experience is possible, that he or she has the ability to relax, think positively, and access positive resources from within (thus interrupting the pattern of negative self-perception that often precludes a recognition of positive personal resources).

Pattern interruption through relaxation and positive input can disrupt the anxiety spiral and allow for the building of self-management skills with self-hypnosis (Lankton & Lankton, 1983), a self-relaxation and self-management process. The effect can be to allow for better sleep and a return to other more normal vegetative functions. Less internal discomfort can alleviate the depressed person's reliance on self-abusive coping patterns involving excessive alcohol, tranquilizers, food, and the like. Discovering one's ability to relax and feel good naturally can have a profound impact on *any* individual, and this is especially true of individuals experiencing depression.

2. Reframing. Reframing through hypnosis may address the client's attitude about his or her experience of depression. Typically, the client views the depression as utterly useless; when viewed in this way, the individual blames him- or herself for having the problem, and for having no ability to control it. This naturally compounds the depression. Herein lies the opportunity for reframing. To reframe seemingly useless depression as a "warning signal that paves the way for an opportunity to change" allows the client to attach positive meaning to a negative experience, altering the person's experience. In fact, depression *is* a warning signal that something is out of balance in the person's world.

Depression may signal a need to redefine a relationship, rethink a decision, alter a thought, feeling or behavior pattern, or change in other ways. Depression is also a natural and healthy outlet for grief and other significant stresses. Reframing depression as a natural and even potentially positive experience can diminish or even eliminate self-blame for the condition. Suggestions for symptom relief and positive lifestyle changes round out the symptomatic approaches.

3. Symptom substitution. Symptom substitution is a third possible pattern of intervention when applying hypnosis for symptom relief. In circumstances where the depression is secondary to serious physical illness (e.g., terminal cancer) and the prognosis is negative, or in circumstances where the depressed individual is somehow unavailable for or unlikely to benefit from more intensive treatment, symptom substitution as a deliberate strategy may be employed. Often the depressed individual somaticizes the symptoms of depression; somatic complaints are more concrete, have more clearly identifiable parameters, and are generally inter- and intrapersonally more acceptable (Suinn, 1984).

Symptom substitution as a strategy may involve the controlled transformation of the emotional pain of depression into an acceptable physical pain, i.e., one that is mild, tolerable, and not disabling. Such a strategy of symptom substitution was described by Erickson (1954a). Somatic complaints where depression is the underlying feature are spontaneous and uncontrolled manifestations of this same process. The key to using this strategy lies in the controlled nature of choosing the site of symptom substitution, thus providing recognition at *some* level of an ability to control the symptom.

Dynamic Approaches

Applying patterns of hypnosis to address the underlying dynamics of the individual's depression is a more demanding and comprehensive means of treatment. A number of hypnotic strategies may be utilized in the course of such treatment, involving various configurations of age regression, age progression, amnesia, catalepsy, dissociation, positive and negative hallucinations, hypermnesia, ideodynamic responses, sensory alteration, and time distortion.

1. Age regression. Regression is a most common vehicle for intervening therapeutically. It seems apparent that learned patterns provide the framework for the depression. Age regression strategies may involve the accessing of positive resources from the past to incorporate into current and future contexts, a pattern well described elsewhere (Lankton & Lankton, 1983; Bandler & Grinder, 1979; Grinder & Bandler, 1981).

Age regression may further involve guiding the client experientially through revivification (Yapko, 1984a) to relive past episodes in which negative generalizations (i.e., cognitive distortions [Beck et al., 1979]) were made. In general, the purpose of the technique is to alter the internal representation of the experience, i.e., the way the memory was incorporated as well as the conclusions drawn from it. In other words, the memory is "reworked" in order to reach new, more adaptive conclusions. The "reworking" may come about from any or all of the following: uncovering repressed memories, providing emotional release, shifting the person's focus from one dimension of the memory to another, helping the person organize present or desired personal resources to use effectively in past experiences (e.g., controlling an uncontrollable event), and using techniques of cognitive restructuring (Beck et al., 1979; Beck, 1983) amplified in power due to the presence of the trance state. Once the memory has been reworked or reframed in this type of "critical incident process" (Yapko, 1984a) where significant events are reexperienced and therapeutically resolved, the new positive feelings and thoughts related to the memory and to the related dimensions of self-image can be "brought back" and integrated with current modes of functioning.

Another dynamic process involving age regression that is effective and versatile is the technique of "changing personal history" (Grinder & Bandler, 1981) involving some patterns similar to those of the "critical incident process" just described. Changing personal history involves guiding the hypnotized client back to earliest memory and providing a structured set of life experiences that unfold over time to "live and learn from." The kinds of experiences to be structured for the individual are those that can provide positive generalizations about one's self and one's life.

The client is encouraged to experience the suggested scenarios fully, and to use all the dimensions of each scenario to its fullest, most positive extent (Lankton & Lankton, 1983). Through a disorientation for time passage, the client can have months or years of experience in a single trance session. Thus, the person can have moving experiences of having the parent that was lost in youth, having significant interactions with others that enhance a strong, positive self-esteem, and so forth.

In order to fully allow for the positive learnings to generalize from the trance experiences to the rest of the individual's life, multiple sessions of changing personal history may be used in conjunction with ample utilization of posthypnotic suggestions concerning ways "these positive memories can be the framework for which current and future choices can be made, for all people use their past learnings to guide their choices." Such a truism allows the suggestion to be more easily incorporated. Amnesia may be selectively utilized to repress specific details of the instilled memories while allowing the positive generalizations derived from them to assume an active role in guiding the person's ongoing experience (Erickson & Rossi, 1979).

2. Age progression. Age progression can be used dynamically in the utilization of hypnotic approaches for depression. A conceptually simple goal is to provide a means for building positive expectations for the future. The hypnotized client is encouraged to experience positive future consequences arising from changes and decisions being made currently. Concurrently, the client can be dissociated from the effects of negative past experiences, making future choices on the basis of current awareness, not negative history.

As with the regression processes, the client is encouraged to fully experience the scenarios and reap the benefits of having taken active and effective steps in his or her own behalf. Thus, generalizations that only the passage of time would make available to the client can be obtained through trance sessions involving age progression, allowing the client to experience a higher degree of confidence that current efforts are worthwhile.

The benefit is not simply the enjoyment of a higher level of confidence, but includes the willingness to actively progress; after all, negative expectation has an immobilizing effect — "Why bother if it's not going to do any good?" Age progression provides an experiential reference point for the belief that making necessary changes *will* do some good.

A second age progression strategy involves orienting the client to the negative consequences of continuing current patterns, i.e., experiencing the effects of remaining ambivalent or immobilized regarding self-help decisions. Considering the degree of ambivalence in the depressed individual, hypnotically facilitating a concrete experience of the negative patterns can provide the client with the momentum needed in order to make positive decisions. Age progression can move distant expectations into the realm of immediate experience. The effect is not unlike Haley's "encouraging the worse alternative" strategy (1973).

A third treatment strategy utilizing age progression is Erickson's "pseudo-orientation in time" (Erickson, 1954b). Through use of dissociation and amnesia, the client is guided experientially into a future context to be experienced as present reality wherein he or she can assess the quality of life, reflect on the changes successfully undergone recently to improve the quality of life, and describe what the stimuli for those changes were. Essentially, the client is providing information regarding the learnings necessary to effect meaningful change and how to facilitate them. The clinician may use this information skillfully to guide the client into scenarios where such learnings may be acquired.

Dissociative patterns of hypnosis are part of the above processes, but a more pure form of dissociation may be effective in addressing dimensions of depression. For example, in the case of one depressed client, suggestions were offered to acknowledge her split feelings and split awarenesses regarding her situation. It was suggested that she acknowledge a part of her that is characterized as "negative" and simultaneously acknowledge a part of her that is characterized as "positive." Each part could be thought of as occupying its own place within her, each with its own unique set of characteristics.

Suggestions were given to concretize these parts, giving them each a place within her on the basis of how accessible she wanted that part to be regardless of past patterns. Positively motivated, she chose to have her dominant side be positive and her nondominant side be negative. She was encouraged to internally dissociate one side from the other, and listen to (i.e., auditorially hallucinate) each side's interpretation of events before reacting.

Suggestions were given about the ability to selectively choose positive or negative interpretations based on what would be most adaptive for the situation and what would be most subjectively pleasing. Experiences were provided hypnotically to deepen the awareness for the positive side's potential influence. Positive interpretations of experience had never had "a voice in matters" before, and as the client became able to respond to her positive side appropriately, her experience of depression lifted. This pattern is structurally similar to the distorted focus on the exclusively negative aspects of experience typical of depression, but the focus is now shifted to positive dimensions of experience to create a more balanced approach to life (since no one's life is good or bad *all* the time).

3. Therapeutic metaphors. A final hypnotic approach that may be used to facilitate recovery from depression involves the use of therapeutic metaphors. Metaphors delivered to the client in trance are able to address the multiple levels of client experience in potentially useful ways. Zeig (1980a) described the practical capacities of metaphors in diagnosis, establishing rapport, making and illustrating a point, suggesting solutions, getting clients to recognize themselves, seeding ideas and increasing motivation, decreasing resistance, and so forth. Lankton & Lankton (1983) elaborated upon the widespread applicability of metaphors, and provided comprehensive guidelines for their construction and delivery. Gordon (1978) and Rosen (1982) also described considerations for the skilled use of metaphors in the treatment process.

Metaphors in the treatment of depression must be carefully designed and delivered, keeping in mind the client's unique world views and range of personal experience. Metaphors often involve the use of other people (past clients, family members, and others significant in one's range of personal experiences) with whom the client can identify and learn from. Metaphors that simply describe other individuals with similar problems who achieved positive results may indirectly suggest the possibility of recovery from depression. These metaphorical suggestions may not be accepted, however, if the client's frame of reference is one of personal helplessness, i.e., "others may succeed but I know *I* can't." Metaphorical intervention such as the use of case histories help therapists keep in mind the powerful nature of one's world view in its ability to maintain current patterns, even dysfunctional ones.

When metaphors take into account clients' principal sources of resistance, they can build positive expectancy and seed ideas about specific changes. These, in turn, can be reinforced with posthypnotic suggestions. Metaphors to build expectancy can be used in the earliest stages of treatment to simply match the person's experience of helplessness and hopelessness. Introducing positive possibilities may be done at this time, but only selectively. Metaphors that involve past experiences of the client in which he or she was able to succeed under difficult or uncertain conditions are generally quite useful.

Conveying ideas in a nonmetaphoric manner may place too much emphasis on the positive possibilities a client "should" consider and may lead a client to suspect that the clinician does not fully appreciate the intensity of his or her pain. This error is most obvious in interventions such as the one characterized in the following exchange.

Client: I'm so depressed. I don't know why, but nothing seems to matter anymore.

Clinician: Well, what do you have to be depressed about? You have a good life. You have a loving husband who cares for you, three beautiful, healthy kids that are doing well, you have a nice home, nice cars, your health which is most important of all, and . . . .

The above example of contradicting the client's reality predictably will have no impact on the client's depression, and may even compound it by causing the individual to blame him- or herself for having the audacity to be depressed when everything should be going well. Metaphors that do adequately accept the client's reality are likely to have therapeutic impact. Thus, using the same example as above, a useful metaphor might begin with:

. . . I worked with another client once who was so unhappy with her life, and she didn't know why . . . on the surface, everything seemed alright in her life . . . she had a nice family, nice possessions, a nice life . . . but she knew that there was something deeper that needed to be addressed . . . and she wasn't sure just what it was . . . not yet . . . but she did know that people can change . . . and that she was someone who could change . . . even though she didn't know how . . . just yet . . . and she was so unsure at first . . . and she had every right to be . . . and her feelings were so uncomfortable to her . . . it seems no one's depression is more uncomfortable than one's own . . . .

In this example, the emphasis is on building rapport through the matching of realities and only brief mention in the form of a truism is made regarding the possibility of change, seeding the idea to be returned to at a later time.

When the relationship with the client is progressing to the point of shifting from matching realities to facilitating new perspectives (Bandler & Grinder, 1979), therapeutic metaphors may be utilized that emphasize the reframing of experience in positive ways, asserting control or abandoning futile attempts to control, accepting or rejecting responsibility and blame, and developing a more flexible and adaptive way of dealing with the experiences of one's life. Metaphors that Erickson used to illustrate the principle of "take charge of your life" are found in Rosen (1982), and other metaphors more generally addressing changes related directly or indirectly to depression can be found in Haley (1973), Lankton and Lankton (1983), and Erickson and Rossi (1979).

Other metaphors may involve descriptions of the various psychosocial models of depression (e.g., Seligman's "learned helplessness" [1973, 1974, 1975, 1983]) and the interesting research leading to their formulations, as well as nonfiction examples (from past clients or elsewhere) of contexts in which these variables are evident. Examples of effective resolution of these variables can be offered. Metaphors may also be derived from the client's own personal history, reviewing and emphasizing past experiences of transforming ignorance to knowledge, weakness to strength, fear to confidence, and so forth. The early learning sets that Erickson used (Zeig, 1980a) in his teachings were representative of this type of approach, emphasizing one's ability to learn from experience and outgrow old limitations. The implicit message is, "You have all the necessary resources to change." Metaphors are a skillful way of making such resources available to the client, an especially important goal for the client experiencing depression.

Hypnotherapeutic Approaches

The utilization of hypnotic patterns in the treatment of depression seems a most fitting style of intervention. The constricted sense of reality typically present in the depressed client is more accessible to the clinician's interventions in the trance state (Watzlawick, 1978). Hypnosis affords the clinician the opportunity to deal with the client on multiple levels simultaneously (Zeig,

1980a; Yapko, 1984a); in the case of depression, this multiple level style of intervention is especially important.

As a final point of interest, Erickson (1980) described another possible use of hypnosis related to depression:

> . . . should it be desired to make a study of the effects of a state of affective depression upon behavior in general, hypnotic subjects can be placed in a state of profound depression which will serve to govern their conduct in any number of ways. At the same time this depression can be removed and direct contrast made between depressed behavior and normal behavior. . . . (p. 10)

From this statement, it is apparent that Erickson recognized the subjective nature of depression, as well as the responsiveness of depressed individuals to the utilization of hypnosis. The hypnotic patterns described in this section are practical approaches derived from these recognitions.

Strategic Approaches

Strategic approaches to the treatment of depression may include the use of behavioral directives. Such directives actively engage the client in an experience that becomes a context for learning something deemed fundamental to recovery. Simply stated, the client is guided into a situation where a high probability exists that he or she will experientially discover a personal resource or valuable concept that will facilitate recovery from depression. (Posthypnotic suggestions to build an association between a learning and a specific context can better assure such outcomes.)

The emphasis in creating effective strategies is on the client's *experiential* discovery of the significant learning. It is often not enough to simply have the client in a "normal" waking state imagine the experience (thereby restricting the experience to a primarily cognitive level and possibly increasing "intellectualization"). The world is experienced on two levels: the *empirical* (sensory-based) and the *symbolic* (the way sensory experience is organized, stored and communicated). Verbal psychotherapies operate primarily on the symbolic level, yet it is the empirical level that is the target of therapeutic intervention.

By employing strategic interventions that bring salient features of the depression (i.e., depressive thoughts, feelings, or behaviors) into play, but in a way that somehow demands they be altered, it is possible to surpass the usual limits of one's subjective experience. These types of strategic intervention are perhaps best used to rapidly and effectively resolve the impasses that so often arise in the push for therapeutic progress.

Strategic interventions can take a variety of forms, including symptom prescriptions, ordeal therapies, behavioral prescriptions or "homework assignments," double-binds, the utilization of resistance, and other patterns the clinician actively promotes. These patterns are described in detail elsewhere (see Haley, 1973, 1984; Watzlawick, 1978; Zeig, 1980a, 1982; Lankton & Lankton, 1983).

Discussed earlier in this paper was the recognition that although there are numerous ways to conceptualize or characterize depression, three interrelated core dynamics are apparent. They are: (1) a distorted sense of personal responsibility; (2) a distorted pattern of blame related to ongoing experience; and (3) a distorted sense of control. How someone manages these three constructs has an exceptionally profound impact on the range of choices available to the individual. The personality, subjective reality, and all that is encompassed by these two terms are overwhelmingly determined by how one perceives one's degree of responsibility, and how one perceives control over one's own experience. Thus, these three variables can serve as the framework for creating and utilizing strategic interventions. In the sections that follow, each variable and other important variables related to it will be discussed. For the sake of relevance and clarity, strategic interventions that address these variables will be presented throughout.

Personal Responsibility

The distorted sense of personal responsibility that is common among depressed individuals is evident in the tendency (however mild or extreme) to assume either too little or too much responsibility for ongoing experience. The depressed client who consistently views him- or herself as a victim of others' insensitivity (i.e., lack of consideration for his or her needs and wants, however covert they may be) is clearly not sufficiently responsible for the events taking place in the relationship. Typically, the person's self-esteem is so poor that he or she is afraid to express feelings, make realistic demands (i.e., set limits), or even disagree with another person out of fear the other person will leave.

In such instances, the client is underresponsible by not being a full half of the relationship. Self-negation is the core in what has been aptly described by Satir (1972) as the "placater" personality style. In such cases, behavioral prescriptions may be effectively used, providing the clinician senses an undercurrent of frustration, anger, and resistance to placating within the client (i.e., passive-aggressiveness, a common feature of depression). If no such undercurrent is perceived, and no rebellion is likely to occur, the use of such prescriptions is not generally indicated.

Behavioral prescriptions may be used to amplify the tendencies of the underresponsible individual to the point where he or she can simply no longer continue on in such an obviously self-defeating way. Ideally, the client will rebel by responsibly asserting his or her individual rights. For example, in the case of the depressed person who self-critically exclaims, "I have no right to feel this way . . . ," the clinician might demand that the client with a sense of inadequate justification *justify everything he or she does* by giving the prescription that the client give at least three rationales for all activities engaged in (e.g., why I wear these clothes, why I drove home this way, why I chose these foods for lunch, and so forth). This prescription is intended to facilitate the more self-determined recognition that "the mere fact that I feel this way is justification enough." Such self-determination and self-acceptance can enhance the depressed individual's impoverished self-esteem.

A second behavioral prescription may be focused on another dimension of this same pattern: the need for approval. The client may be directed to *ask for permission* to do whatever he or she would like to do (e.g., would it be alright if I went to the bathroom now? Can I get myself a drink of water? Is it alright that I wear these clothes?). This prescription is intended to promote the recognition that "I can do as I wish." Thus, the cycle of self-sacrifice to get others' approval can give way to a pattern of self-approval.

A third behavioral prescription may also be used to address a dynamic that is commonly underlying the tendency to be underresponsible: the fear of making a mistake and visibly being responsible for it. Prescribing that the client *deliberately plan and execute a specified number of mistakes each day* can have the effect of teaching the client that making mistakes is not horrendously unnatural nor is it necessarily catastrophic. Watzlawick (1978, pp. 136–7) described this very intervention in one of his case presentations. Frankl (Davison & Neale, 1982) further described patterns of "paradoxical intention" that are structurally similar.

In each of the above behavioral prescriptions, the client is instructed to carry out a behavior that is a distilled and exaggerated form of a dysfunctional pattern evident in his or her lifestyle. The goal in assigning such behaviors is to mobilize a rejecting attitude against irresponsibly denying oneself in order to gain another's approval. Mobilizing resistance in this way can help build self-esteem, increase recognition of personal choice, establish the validity of one's own preferences, and decrease dependency on others' reactions as the guiding force for one's actions. Assertiveness-training exercises are useful for similar reasons.

In the case of the *overresponsible* individual, the person has created the dysfunctional illusion of responsibility for all the things that go on around him or her. It is unfortunate that the issue of overresponsibility is often fostered in awareness groups that promote the idea that "whatever goes on around you is a reflection of you; you created all of your circumstances." Since this is true only in part, behavioral prescriptions may be used to drive home the point that one cannot be responsible for *everything*. For example, a client may be instructed to clip out newspaper or magazine articles of tragedies (e.g., earthquakes, floods, plane crashes) and give at least three rationales for *how he or she directly or indirectly caused that to happen*.

Over time, the recognition can be encouraged that there are some things one would like to control, but cannot. This seems easy to understand, yet even mental health professionals are notoriously bad at avoiding overresponsibility in relation to their clients, resulting in a high rate of depression, suicide, and substance abuse within the profession (Laliotis & Grayson, 1985). One can easily understand how difficult resolving this issue must be for the layperson when even professionals are unclear about it. Setting the client up to experientially discover the limits of his or her responsibility can be very therapeutic.

Resolving the ambiguity about what one is and is not responsible for is a vital part of the overall treatment of depression. Certainly, a key symptom of depression associated with this issue of responsibility is the excessive guilt suffered by depressed individuals. Does guilt not presuppose responsibility? In a significant number of instances, the depressed client will miss opportunities to help him- or herself because of the overresponsibility associated with guilt.

An example of this is a 26-year-old woman who consulted the author for treatment of depression. She knew what she wanted and needed to do to help herself, but could not because of paralyzing guilt. She wanted to move out of her parents' home and live independently, but she was afraid "it will kill my parents."

In another instance of overresponsibility, a woman seen by the author presented the complaint of depression manifesting itself in instances where she saw others' misfortunes. She would literally burst into tears if she saw a motorist on the side of the road with a flat tire, so diffuse were her personal boundaries.

In both examples, the clients were personalizing responsibility for situations or people they *could* not be responsible for. Feeling responsible for the actions, thoughts, and feelings of another person is a precursor to guilt, causes excessive stress, and has the indirect effect of encouraging others to not be responsible for themselves (which is what continues the common pattern of an overresponsible person in a relationship with an underresponsible person). The consequences include dependency, poor self-esteem, negative expectations, anger, and other depressive symptoms.

A behavioral prescription that may be employed in addressing the social level of depression relative to responsibility is to direct the partners in a close relationship to conduct an extensive "trust walk." This approach can be useful when responsibility is unevenly distributed between the partners. Person A is blindfolded and led around by person B who is totally responsible for A's guidance, a condition that gets very tiresome very quickly. Continuing on past the point of fatigue with the exercise creates a powerful and easily referenced memory of the burden of overresponsibility as well as the burden of underresponsibility. Both parties may play both roles, the role opposite their role in the relationship, or the role that parallels their role in the relationship. There is something valuable to be learned from each vantage point.

Patterns of Blame

Zeig (personal communication, 1984) described one dimension of client patterns worthy of assessment as "intrapunitive vs. extrapunitive," referring to one's tendency to blame and punish oneself vs. others. All people necessarily make attributions of responsibility for their subjective experiences, attributing the event's etiology first to an internal or external cause, and then to a more specific source of responsibility for that event.

When one assumes little or no responsibility for one's own thoughts, actions, or behaviors, one becomes extrapunitive, i.e., blames others for one's own circumstances. Recognition of responsibility for one's own choices is marginal in such instances. When one assumes too much responsibility, the tendency is to become intrapunitive, i.e., blaming oneself for one's inability to make everything alright, regardless of whether or not the power objectively exists to do so.

Attribution of blame for one's circumstances is a variable that takes different forms in the instance of depression. Certainly the concept of "learned helplessness" (specifically "personal helplessness") is relevant here, an instance where one blames uncontrollable external events for one's depressed condition. The model of depression involving "anger turned inward" also addresses the issue of blame, from the perspective of blaming oneself for the frustrations and inequities of life.

Behavioral prescriptions involving dynamics of blame may be used to shift the burden of responsibility for an event to where it belongs. For example, with one inappropriately self-blaming member of a couple seeking treatment, the author instructed the wife to make a list of 10 significant negative historical events occurring prior to her birth. She was told to attempt to convince her husband that she was to blame for these events (such as Lincoln's assassination), and to be as convincing as possible in her admissions of guilt. The effect was dramatic. So easily could the woman be to blame for ongoing events that she shocked herself with how guilty she could feel about events occurring long before her birth!

In a related prescription reversing the pattern, the client may be asked to make a list of personal accomplishments, and then deny having anything to do with any of them. In a variation of this pattern, the client can be instructed to carry out assigned behaviors, and then immediately offer excuses for the outcome of those behaviors (i.e., "well, the lighting was bad, and I hadn't had lunch, and I had a hangnail, and mom always liked my brother better, and . . . "). In the use of such seemingly lighthearted interventions, the issue of ascribing blame comes to the fore and a "placater" or "blamer" (Satir, 1972) may for the first time get a glimpse of him- or herself long enough to interrupt the pattern.

In a symptom prescription strategy, the other-blaming client may be told to blame others—constantly. Rather than risking whatever social life the individual might have, the client is instructed to "blame out loud" for specified periods of time when others are not around. For example, when driving alone, the client may be told to loudly "curse everything and everyone for not doing things the right way." The client is encouraged to blame others for being so stupid as to drive a different make and color car, or for being young or old, or for putting a building in a particular spot, and on and on. Maintaining the hostile, blaming demeanor soon gets very tiresome.

In another example of a symptom prescription of sorts, a 57-year-old seriously depressed woman who had just suffered the loss of her husband of 35 years presented herself to the author for treatment. Since his death, she had not left her home, terrified to emerge as an independent adult. She had been married to the "perfect husband who took care of me completely." She had never had to fill her own car with gas, had never had to make a bank deposit, never had to do many of the errands most people do routinely. Her overresponsible husband's death left her totally unable to manage her own life independently—he had, in effect, killed her with kindness.

In an early stage of treatment, the client was encouraged to express her resentment about his death and to bitterly blame him for dying. Quite emotionally, she did so. Somewhere in the midst of her hurling blame at him, it dawned on her that "it probably wasn't his idea to die . . . " Encouraging the blame allowed her to stop the blaming and begin working on her acquiring the skills necessary to live life competently.

Self-blame is not unlike the self-sacrifice of martyrdom that can clearly have a manipulative quality in its implicit message that "I'll be the scapegoat so you don't have to bear the burden of guilt . . . and what will you do for me?" When such a pattern is observed by the clinician, prescribing episodes of martyrdom can be utilized. Placing the client's body in a position of someone on a crucifix while moaning, "After all I've done for you, how can you do this to me?" with relevant personal examples can afford one a lighter glimpse at a serious pattern.

A prescription in which family members are instructed to continually blame the self-blaming client for whatever happens (e.g., rain, unemployment figures, a damaged wheat crop) can mobilize that person's resistance and lead him or her to assert blamelessness. Such assertion is a necessary step in recognizing the limits of one's responsibility; such lines are so often blurred when depression is present. In an example of this type of pattern, an attorney in his mid-40s who was quite successful despite a chronic, moderate depression was made the "scapegoat" for the family. He was all too experienced with being blamed for things, based on his having very critical, rejecting parents. This was a pattern his family continued to carry out. Absurd blaming statements heaped on him by his family were to be met only with the reply, "Please forgive me."

After a few days of experiencing this prescription that everyone initially found amusing, the client became enraged and firmly declared his inability to experience any more blame for anyone unless he either first acknowledged the blame as properly his or else was approached in a more neutral "let's talk about it" sort of manner. This was the start of a considerably more functional way of managing the issue of blame and all the related self-esteem factors.

A common reframing method that addresses the issue of blame is the often-quoted philosophy commonly related to Ericksonian approaches: the client is always making the best choices he or she has, given the range of available resources (Bandler & Grinder, 1979; Lankton, 1980). An "error" becomes "the best choice available."

An ordeal that deliberately involves self-punishment in one form or another whenever blame is inappropriately ascribed may be a useful intervention. For example, Haley (1984) described a depressed man who was told to either find a job within a week or shave off his highly prized mustache. Blame for prior lack of ambition to work was an issue bypassed when the ordeal succeeded. Demanding that clients perform tasks that are more arduous than letting go of their symptoms can be a viable therapeutic strategy. In such instances, dealing directly with the blame for the situation is unnecessary in order to obtain a therapeutic result. However, caution is advised in the use of such ordeal strategies, for although the presenting problem may be ingeniously resolved, the client may not learn how to generalize appropriate management of blame to other contexts (Yapko, 1983).

The Locus of Control

The author has repeatedly observed in his depressed clients a confusion relative to the issue of "control." Specifically, the depressed individual is lacking clarity in his or her ability to determine what is and what is not within the range of meaningful influence (Phares, 1984; Seligman, 1973, 1974, 1975).

Consequently, either the person attempts to exert control over events that are objectively uncontrollable (e.g., a traffic jam at rush hour), or the individual makes no apparent attempt to control events that are objectively controllable (e.g., seeking new employment when the current work situation is somehow detrimental). When the issue of control is one that is muddled for the client, interventions may be designed to promote a refined awareness for the distinctions between controllable and uncontrollable events. With such an awareness, the client can be prevented from assuming a position of "personal helplessness" both by recognizing a wider variety of conditions of "universal helplessness" and by empowering him- or herself to effectively deal with situations perceived as controllable.

In many instances, depression is a reaction to discovering the uncontrollable nature of something important to the person. In one woman the author treated, the presenting complaint of depression was in large part a reaction to her son's refusal to attend medical school, as she was so set on his being a physician. Clearly, she was attempting to control her son, whom she could not control, since he was making competent decisions on his own. Therapy involved developing acceptance for his ability to decide what his own life should be about, and began with the reframing: "How wonderful a mother you must have been in raising him to have him turn out so clear about who he is and what he wants." She had not yet seen it that way, and this guiding perspective made the rest of our work considerably easier.

Behavioral prescriptions may be used to amplify the distorted nature of the depressed individual's thought that "I should be able to control this" when it exists in reference to something perceived by the clinician as objectively uncontrollable. When the issue of control has been discussed to whatever extent is desirable with a given individual, the client may be directed to attempt to deliberately exert control over something already recognized as universally uncontrollable, such as the weather, the outcome of a sporting event, or some other such event. The client can be encouraged to use whatever methods he or she chooses (desperate pleas, etc.) to influence the outcome, acting "as if" it could make a difference. Such a role play has had the effect with many clients of bringing true feelings of frustration and anger to the surface that had lain dormant, providing the opportunity for therapeutic resolution.

In a related assignment, the client may be directed to carefully observe the techniques of skilled manipulators who attempt to influence the thoughts, feelings and behaviors of others. The television evangelist has been a favorite example used by the author. The typical, forcefully stated presuppositions of moral righteousness mixed with techniques of manipulation involving fear and guilt are used to attempt to gain control of the lives of others. By actively and critically viewing the evangelist's use of negative manipulation tactics, the client may externalize (i.e., see as if outside oneself) his or her similar patterns and thus dissociate from them.

Simply stated, the internal emotional havoc related to depression that arises from trying to control uncontrollable events comes from the focus on one's anger, guilt, emotional distance, disappointment, and other feelings that are typically other-directed. The above example of the depressed mother is a typical example of intense anger and disappointment being focused on her son, who, if he had been a less secure young man, might have felt guilty for his mother's reaction and then complied with her wishes.

"Instrumental depression" is a term coined by the author to describe episodes of depression whose manipulative value is a key feature of its onset. In this case, the mother was encouraged to actively view the evangelists and their techniques for getting compliance with no regard for the emotional price (in guilt and fear) paid by those who comply. This "get me what I want at any cost" pattern violates the most basic of assumptions about personal integrity associated with Ericksonian approaches. Respecting another person's choice, even if contrary to one's own, is considered mandatory. The net effect on the woman, in combination with the reframing described earlier, was to promote a comfortable recognition that people can be allowed to make their own best choices for themselves. Presupposing that one is better able to judge what is good for someone than that individual is able to do for him- or herself is a pattern highly likely to lead to power struggles one cannot win.

To make the point even more overt, the therapist may direct the client to choose an unimportant issue to "crusade" about for a specified amount of time. The rejecting or indifferent attitudes encountered relative to even an unimportant issue can teach the client experientially how attempting to control others' thoughts, feelings and actions is wasted energy.

Each of the strategies described thus far is intended to drive home the point that one cannot control others, and that the sooner one learns that, the sooner one will end the spiral involving anger, frustration, and depression. Further intervention can be focused on helping the client to generalize the recognition of the uncontrollable nature of people to the uncontrollable nature of other specific events.

The other side of this issue concerns the problem of not controlling things that *are* controllable. The "learned helplessness" model of Seligman (1973, 1975) suggests a gradual behavioral shaping strategy in dealing with depressed individuals evidencing this dynamic. Designing a series of tasks that can be successfully accomplished can build a positive momentum toward establishing the generalization that one can set a goal and actively progress toward its accomplishment.

Symptom prescriptions may be effectively used to facilitate an awareness for the control of seemingly uncontrollable experiences. For example, prescribing the symptom of depression by establishing a scheduled "depression time" can allow the client to deliberately and masterfully create the experience instead of being its passive victim. Similarly, prescribing that the client "be passive," "be whiney," "be negative," and so forth for specified and inconvenient periods of time can mobilize a considerable resistance to having those experiences.

Prescribing helplessness, in particular, can mobilize the "I'm *not* helpless" discovery. For example, the client can be encouraged to ask for direction to do things and go places already well known to him or her. The effect can be to mobilize the feeling of "Why should I wait for directions to do what I know I can do?" Encouraging the client to passively wait for things to be done for him or her can also mobilize the frustration of waiting for others and point the way to an independent solution. In one behavioral prescription, for example, a client was instructed to wait for others to open all doors for her, including her doors at home (even though she lived alone!). If, after two minutes, no one helped her, only then could she open it for herself. She had progressively stronger reactions during the many two-minute periods of passive waiting that followed, and when the negative reaction to passivity became very intense after several days, she developed a strong awareness of ways she had been passive to a fault. This awareness became an excellent resource for later sessions that emphasized taking greater control over her experience.

Any strategy that turns the depressing paralysis of ambivalence in a positive direction will also facilitate the recognition of one's ability to make decisions in one's own behalf. Ambivalence is conceptualized by the author as an overt manifestation of not controlling the controllable. The "approach-avoidance" conflict describes ambivalence in part, but clinical experience leads the author to believe that the client is *not* so genuinely mixed in feeling as much as he or she is fearful of committing to a course of action. The client knows what he or she wants, but does not sense the power or the right to have it.

Erickson's strategy of "encouraging the worse alternative" (Haley, 1973) is a good one to get movement in an otherwise motionless client's decision-making process. By encouraging the alternative least desirable to the client unable or unwilling to make a decision, the client's resistance to that directive encourages movement in the direction of the other, better alternative. Use of metaphors that illustrate the "he who hesitates is lost" truism (e.g., stories of missed opportunities arising from indecision) can also encourage making the transition from passive to active in one's own behalf.

Recreational approaches that encourage the depressed client to do enjoyable things are behavioral prescriptions that can lead the client to discover important insights. Such recreational therapy approaches make the point that "if you don't do things you enjoy doing, how can you expect to ever feel good?" Furthermore, the client discovers a self-controlled and reliable way to "get outside of oneself" (out of the depressive internal focus), a shift which can have great therapeutic value. Giving the behavioral assignment to list 20 or

30 enjoyable recreational activities can help the client organize a concrete list to refer to for things to do during periods of depression when anhedonia and apathy are otherwise likely to set in. Recreational activities mobilize positive energy, demand involvement, relieve stress, and give one mastery over one's own time. The key in addressing "helplessness" is to gently force the client to contradict his or her depressive generalizations, and to provide new positive stimuli in order to build greater recognition of the ever-present range of personal choices one can make in one's own best interest.

Contraindications

Due to the serious nature of depression, particularly the potential for suicide, the various hypnotic and strategic interventions described in this chapter must be chosen and utilized with careful attention to the individual client's nature. Many of the patterns presented here have been intended to mobilize the resistance of a client against his or her own depression-maintaining patterns or to the demands of the clinician. Such patterns presuppose the existence of such resistance in the individual. However, clinicians *cannot* assume the presence of such resistance. Depending on the individual, the resistance may be too weak, or too deeply buried beneath depressive patterns to be effectively mobilized. In many instances, extensive supportive psychotherapy is indicated before such interventions as those described here may be effectively used. If the timing of these interventions is misjudged, these interventions can actually be antitherapeutic. For example, in a hospital setting the author observed a psychotherapist attempt a provocative "aggression training" therapy on a depressed patient. In such an approach, the concept of depression as "anger turned inward" is the framework for the intervention, and the intervention attempts to so anger a patient that he or she will turn the anger outward again, and blow up angrily, with a therapeutic effect.

In this case, the clinician demanded that the patient scrub the hallway with a toothbrush. After several hours of the patient's scrubbing on hands and knees, the clinician returned and began to defiantly and deliberately scuff the scrubbed floor with his heels. Instead of the patient getting angry, he simply sighed and further withdrew. The intervention obviously was inappropriate for that patient, a destructive miscalculation on the part of the therapist. If there is any doubt as to the likelihood of an intervention being appropriate for a depressed client, then it is more conservative and respectful to not use such an intervention.

Summary

As the stresses of people's more and more complicated lives continue to increase, it is predictable that episodes of depression will increase as well. Depression distorts perceptions and so negatively skews the direction of one's life that it may be the most insidious of all disorders. The threat of suicide is ever present in working with depressed clients. Suicide has been called "the permanent solution to temporary problems"; the threat of suicide, as well as the deep pain of depression, necessitates the development of a wide variety of interventions varying in directiveness and in involvement of the multiple levels of the problem. When deemed appropriate after careful consideration, patterns of hypnosis and strategic psychotherapy can be most effective in facilitating escape from the chains of depression.

References

ABRAMSON, L., SELIGMAN, M., & TEASDALE, J. (1978). Learned helplessness in humans: Critique and reformulation. *Journal of Abnormal Psychology, 87,* 49–74.

ALEXANDER, L. (1982). Erickson's approach to hypnotic psychotherapy of depression. In J. Zeig (Ed.), *Ericksonian approaches to hypnosis and psychotherapy* (pp. 219–227). New York: Brunner/Mazel.

AMERICAN PSYCHIATRIC ASSOCIATION. (1980). *Diagnostic and statistical manual of mental disorders* (3rd ed.). Washington, DC: Author.

ARONSON, E. (1984). *The Social Animal* (4th ed.). New York: Freeman.

BANDLER, R. & GRINDER, J. (1975). *The structure of magic* (Vol. 1). Palo Alto, CA: Science & Behavior Books.

BANDLER, R. & GRINDER, J. (1979). *Frogs into princes.* Moab, UT: Real People Press.

BECK, A. (1967). *Depression.* New York: Harper & Row.

BECK, A. (1973). *The diagnosis and management of depression.* Philadelphia: University of Pennsylvania Press.

BECK, A. (1983). Negative cognitions. In E. Levitt, B. Lubin & J. Brooks (Eds.), *Depression: Concepts, controversies, and some new facts* (2nd ed.) (pp. 86–92). Hillsdale, NJ: Erlbaum.

BECK, A., RUSH, J., SHAW, B., & EMERY, G. (1979). *Cognitive therapy of depression.* New York: Guilford Press.

BURNS, D. (1980). *Feeling good: The new mood therapy.* New York: Morrow.

DAVISON, G. & NEALE, J. (1982). *Abnormal psychology* (3rd ed.). New York: Wiley.

ERICKSON, M. (1954a). Special techniques of brief hypnotherapy. *Journal of Clinical and Experimental Hypnosis, 2,* 109–129.

ERICKSON, M. (1954b). Pseudo-orientation in time as a hypnotherapeutic procedure. *Journal of Clinical and Experimental Hypnosis, 2,* 261–283.

ERICKSON, M. (1980). The applications of hypnosis to psychiatry. In E. Rossi (Ed.),

The collected papers of Milton H. Erickson on hypnosis (Vol. IV) (pp. 3–13). New York: Irvington.

ERICKSON, M. & ROSSI, E. (1979). *Hypnotherapy: An exploratory casebook.* New York: Irvington.

FRANKL, V. (1963) *Man's search for meaning.* New York: Washington Square Press.

GIBSON, J. (1983). *Living: Human development through the lifespan.* Reading, MA: Addison-Wesley.

GORDON, D. (1978). *Therapeutic metaphors.* Cupertino, CA: Meta Publications.

GRINDER, J. & BANDLER, R. (1981). *Trance-formations.* Moab, UT: Real People Press.

HALEY, J. (1973). *Uncommon therapy.* New York: Norton.

HALEY, J. (1984). *Ordeal therapy.* San Francisco: Jossey-Bass.

HARLOW, H. & SUOMI, S. (1974). Induced depression in monkeys. *Behavioral Biology, 12,* 273–296.

KLEINMUNTZ, B. (1980). *Essentials of abnormal psychology* (2nd ed.). New York: Harper & Row.

KOLB, L. & BRODIE, H. (1982). *Modern clinical psychiatry* (10th ed.). Philadelphia: W. B. Saunders.

LALIOTIS, D. & GRAYSON, J. (1985). Psychologist heal thyself. *American Psychologist, 40,* 84–96.

LANKTON, S. (1980). *Practical magic.* Cupertino, CA: Meta Publications.

LANKTON, S. & LANKTON, C. (1983). *The answer within: A clinical framework of Ericksonian hypnotherapy.* New York: Brunner/Mazel.

MAHONEY, M. (1980). *Abnormal psychology: Perspectives on human variance.* New York: Harper & Row.

MILLER, H. (1984). Depression: A specific cognitive pattern. In W. Webster (Ed.), *Clinical hypnosis: A multidisciplinary approach* (2nd ed.) (pp. 421–458). Philadelphia: Lippincott.

PHARES, E. (1984). *Introduction to personality.* Columbus, OH: Charles Merrill.

ROSEN, S. (1982). *My voice will go with you: The teaching tales of Milton H. Erickson.* New York: Norton.

SARASON, I. & SARASON, B. (1980). *Abnormal psychology* (3rd ed.). Englewood Cliffs, NJ: Prentice-Hall.

SATIR, V. (1972). *Peoplemaking.* Palo Alto, CA: Science & Behavior Books.

SECUNDA, S., FRIEDMAN, R., & SCHUYLER, D. (1973). *The depressive disorders: Special report, 1973.* (DHEW Publication No. HSM-73-9157). Washington, DC: U.S. Government Printing Office.

SELIGMAN, M. (1973). Fall into helplessness. *Psychology Today,* June 7, 43–48.

SELIGMAN, M. (1974). Depression and learned helplessness. In R. Friedman & M. Katz (Eds.), *The psychology of depression: Contemporary theory and research.* Washington, DC: Winston.

SELIGMAN, M. (1975). *Helplessness: On depression, development, and death.* New York: Freeman.

SELIGMAN, M. (1983). Learned helplessness. In E. Levitt, B. Lubin, & J. Brooks (Eds.), *Depression: Concepts, controversies, and some new facts* (2nd ed.) (pp. 64–72). Hillsdale, NJ: Erlbaum.

SPIEGEL, H. & SPIEGEL, D. (1978). *Trance and treatment: Clinical uses of hypnosis.* New York: Basic Books.

SUINN, R. (1984). *Fundamentals of abnormal psychology.* Chicago: Nelson-Hall, Inc.

WATZLAWICK, P. (1976). *How real is real?* New York: Vintage Books.

WATZLAWICK, P. (1978). *The language of change.* New York: Basic Books.
YAPKO, M. (1981). The effect of matching primary representational system predicates on hypnotic relaxation. *American Journal of Clinical Hypnosis, 23,* 169–175.
YAPKO, M. (1983). A comparative analysis of direct and indirect hypnotic communication styles. *American Journal of Clinical Hypnosis, 25,* 270–276.
YAPKO, M. (1984a). *Trancework: An introduction to clinical hypnosis.* New York: Irvington.
YAPKO, M. (1984b). Implications of the Ericksonian and Neuro-Linguistic Programming approachs for responsibility of therapeutic outcomes. *American Journal of Clinical Hypnosis, 27,* 137–143.
YAPKO, M. (1985). The Erickson hook: Values in Ericksonian approaches. In J. Zeig (Ed.), *Ericksonian psychotherapy* (Vol. I) (pp. 266–281). New York: Brunner/ Mazel.
ZEIG, J. (Ed.). (1980a). *A teaching seminar with Milton H. Erickson.* New York: Brunner/Mazel.
ZEIG, J. (1980b). Symptom prescription techniques: Clinical applications using elements of communication. *American Journal of Clinical Hypnosis, 23,* 23–33.
ZEIG, J. (Ed.). (1982). *Ericksonian approaches to hypnosis and psychotherapy.* New York: Brunner/Mazel.
ZEIG, J. (Ed.). (1985). *Ericksonian psychotherapy* (2 Vols.). New York: Brunner/ Mazel.

An Instrument
for Utilizing Client Interests
and Individualizing Hypnosis

D. Corydon Hammond, Ph.D.

A distinguishing feature of Milton Erickson's work was his emphasis on in-dividualizing hypnosis and psychotherapy through careful treatment planning. A review is presented of the manner in which he utilized the background in-terests, life experiences, personality needs, and cognitive sets of patients. However, the therapist's ability to follow Erickson's model is often limited by the lack of background information about the patient.

A method is presented for using a checklist as an aid in facilitating Ericksonian assessment and treatment planning. Indications and contraindications for the use of the instrument are provided. Then examples are presented about the use of the checklist in collecting information that facilitates therapist creativity and assists in individualizing inductions, deepening techniques, metaphors, posthypnotic suggestions, and symbolic techniques, and in eliciting hypnotic phenomena.

A distinguishing feature of Milton Erickson was his emphasis on individualiz-ing hypnosis and psychotherapy. Since his pioneering work, this approach has now become a well-accepted clinical practice and there is tentative research support (e.g., Nuland & Field, 1970; Holroyd, 1980) for the belief that hyp-nosis is most effective when it is individualized to the patient. In the field of psychotherapy, in fact, there is evidence that failure to individualize therapy may result in poor outcome and even psychological casualties (Lieberman, Yalom & Miles, 1973).

Rather than using a standardized approach with all patients, Erickson

Address reprint requests to: D. Corydon Hammond, Ph.D., University Medical Center, 50 North Medical Drive, Salt Lake City, Utah 84132.

(Rossi, 1980, Vol. 1, pp. 168–176) encouraged the utilization of the background interests, needs and motivations of the patient. Under his influence, hypnosis has moved away from the concept of externally imposing suggestions and toward his utilization model of accessing inner resources. He believed "that the patient has resources in his personal history that can be used to effect change" (Rossi, 1980, Vol. 2, p. 337).

Erickson provided many rich examples of how to utilize patient interests hypnotically. For example, in treating a man who enjoyed music (Haley, 1973), Erickson carefully learned the specific songs that this patient had recently enjoyed, and "every effort was made to fit their titles, or quotations from them, into therapeutic suggestions" (p. 131).

There are a number of other instances when Erickson utilized the musical interests of patients. In treating a musician with sweating palms (Erickson & Rossi, 1979, pp. 150, 162), he incorporated her musical interests into the trance induction and later used them as a distraction to facilitate amnesia. Before Erickson began formulating a treatment plan for a patient with a problem of excessive modesty (Rossi, 1980, Vol. 4, p. 356), he identified some of her interests: "As a possible clue to a method of approach, she was asked, among other things, if she had ever done any painting or sketching, and if she had ever seen or done any ballet dancing" (p. 358). Upon learning that she played piano and had practiced ballet, music and dancing were incorporated into her initial hypnotic induction and subsequent treatment.

In another case, Erickson (Rossi, 1980, Vol. 4, p. 470) utilized a woman's knowledge of nursery tales to formulate posthypnotic suggestions and help her change her self-image. When he worked with a terminally ill patient who was "highly addicted to television," Erickson taught her to dissociate from pain, leaving her body in bed while she watched her favorite television shows in the living room (Erickson & Rossi, 1979, p. 140). Erickson identified "what pleasures do you like" (Erickson & Rossi, 1979, p. 368), and then utilized them.

An innovation by Erickson was his practice of interspersing suggestions in a metaphor or conversation. When asked what principles he used in formulating multiple levels of communication (Erickson & Rossi, 1981), Erickson replied, "You have to know enough about the other person, especially their interests" (p. 27). Thus when he (Rossi, 1980, Vol. 4, pp. 262–278) treated a retired farmer and florist with cancer pain, he discussed growing plants to intersperse and conceal suggestions. In treating a woman invested in being a mother, he talked about caring for children (Erickson & Rossi, 1976, p. 275).

Erickson also incorporated patient values and beliefs into hypnotic inductions and suggestions. Although he was personally not actively involved in religion, he was more than willing to utilize the religious beliefs and values of his patients (e.g., Haley, 1973, p. 126; Rossi, 1980, Vol. 2, p. 203).

A Method for Ericksonian Assessment & Treatment Planning

Erickson's utilization approach requires that assessment involve much more than the usual background history or psychological testing that is so common in psychotherapy. Assessment is a process of also becoming personally acquainted with the patient and learning about details that may, to some non-Ericksonian clinicians, seem mundane and irrelevant. Lankton and Lankton (1983) have thoughtfully identified a variety of parameters that Erickson considered in treatment planning: availability of resources, flexibility, the developmental age or task of the patient, self-image, the adaptive function of the symptom, structure of the family system and social network, and the stage of family development.

Zeig (1980) stressed the importance in Ericksonian assessment of noting degree of absorption, level of control in relationships, responsiveness to indirect versus direct suggestions, and whether the patient is more internal or external in his focus of attention. Erickson even paid careful attention to the linguistic patterns and phraseology which patients used, so he could use their semantic patterns in induction and suggestion (Erickson & Rossi, 1976, p. 29).

Erickson described, in part, his assessment process: "In the initial interview, the therapist gathers the relevant facts regarding the patient's problems and the *repository of life experiences and learnings that will be utilized for therapeutic purposes*" (Erickson & Rossi, 1979, p. 2). "The therapist can explore patient's personal histories, character, and emotional dynamics, their field of work, interests, hobbies, and so on to assess the range of life experiences and response abilities that may be available for achieving therapeutic goals" (p. 2).

In the remainder of this paper, I will describe an innovative method that I use to collect information that I utilize in my approach to hypnosis.

Checklist for Utilizing Life Experiences

One of the important legacies from Erickson is his emphasis on careful treatment planning. However, a frequent impediment to individualization is lack of information. Considerable information about the interests and life experiences of patients may be gathered casually during interviews. However, there are limits to the amount of time that clinicians can spend in such discussion.

The *Checklist for Utilizing Life Experiences, Interests and Values* (see pp. 114–116) I developed as an aid in collecting a greater amount of information

Checklist for Utilizing
Life Experiences, Interests and Values

Copyright © 1982, 1984, D. Corydon Hammond, Ph.D.
University of Utah School of Medicine

Name: _____   Date: _____

Instructions: This is a checklist of experiences and interests that many people have had. It will help us better understand and appreciate you as an individual. In the space beside each item **which you have experienced**, please rate the degree to which you have liked or enjoyed (past or present) the activity on a scale of **1** to **7**. The number **7** represents something that you love or enjoy very much, and the number **1** represents something that you have strongly disliked. A rating of **4** signifies that you feel neutral about the item. If you liked or disliked something in the past and this has now changed more than two numbers, you can give two ratings and write "past" or "now" beside the different number ratings. Leave items blank that are not in your background of experience.

_____ 1.	Acting in a play	_____ 26. Christmas eve or morning
_____ 2.	Afraid of failing in school	_____ 27. Circus
_____ 3.	Amusement park rides	_____ 28. Climbing a tree
_____ 4.	Anesthesia	_____ 29. Coloring books
_____ 5.	Aquarium/watching fish	_____ 30. Comic books
_____ 6.	Archery	_____ 31. Cooking
_____ 7.	Attending church	_____ 32. Creative writing
_____ 8.	Ballet	_____ 33. Creeks or rivers
_____ 9.	Bedtime stories/fairy tales	_____ 34. Dancing
_____ 10.	Best friend moving away	_____ 35. Death of a loved one
_____ 11.	Bicycle riding	_____ 36. Death of a pet
_____ 12.	Bird watching	_____ 37. Deep sea fishing
_____ 13.	Blowing bubbles	_____ 38. Dinner in a restaurant
_____ 14.	Boating	_____ 39. Diving in a swimming pool
_____ 15.	Body building (with weights)	_____ 40. Doodling
_____ 16.	Bowling	_____ 41. Drug use
_____ 17.	Broken arm/leg	_____ 42. Electric trains
_____ 18.	Building a snowman	_____ 43. Elevators
_____ 19.	Bullied	_____ 44. Embarrassed by acne
_____ 20.	Camping out	_____ 45. Embarrassed in front of a group
_____ 21.	Candlelight	_____ 46. Escalators
_____ 22.	Canoeing or rowboating	_____ 47. Exercising
_____ 23.	Card playing	_____ 48. Feeding the birds
_____ 24.	Carpentry/woodworking	_____ 49. Feeling awkward on dates
_____ 25.	Carving	_____ 50. Feeling left out

Packets of the *Checklist for Utilizing Life Experiences, Interests and Values* may be ordered from the author for $5.00 (which includes postage and mailing) for each packet of 25. Make checks payable to the author and order from: D. Corydon Hammond, Ph.D., University Medical Center, Salt Lake City, Utah 84132.

_____ 51. Feeling unattractive

_____ 52. Fishing

_____ 53. Flying an airplane

_____ 54. Flying in an airplane

_____ 55. Flying a kite

_____ 56. Fog

_____ 57. Gambling

_____ 58. Gardening

_____ 59. Gliding

_____ 60. Going barefoot

_____ 61. Going for a drive

_____ 62. Going to a party

_____ 63. Going to the dentist

_____ 64. Going to the zoo

_____ 65. Golf

_____ 66. Grandfather clocks

_____ 67. Gymnastics

_____ 68. Halloween

_____ 69. Hang gliding

_____ 70. Having a collection (coins, etc.)

_____ 71. Hiking

_____ 72. Hockey

_____ 73. Hopscotch

_____ 74. Horseback riding

_____ 75. Hot tub or jacuzzi

_____ 76. Hunting

_____ 77. Ice skating

_____ 78. Inpatient surgery

_____ 79. Jogging

_____ 80. Jumping rope

_____ 81. Karate/judo/aikido

_____ 82. Knit/crochet

_____ 83. Lakes or reservoirs

_____ 84. Last chosen for a team

_____ 85. Listening to music

_____ 86. Lived in a rural (farm) area

_____ 87. Looking at the stars and moon

_____ 88. Lovemaking/sex

_____ 89. Lying in a hammock

_____ 90. Making a snow sculpture

_____ 91. Mechanics work

_____ 92. Meditation

_____ 93. Motorcycle riding

_____ 94. Movies

_____ 95. Not asked out for dates

_____ 96. Nursing a baby

_____ 97. Ocean cruise

_____ 98. Operations

_____ 99. Overweight

_____ 100. Painting/sketching

_____ 101. Pets (dogs, cats, etc.)

_____ 102. Picnics

_____ 103. Pillow fight

_____ 104. Ping pong

_____ 105. Pipe smoking

_____ 106. Playing a musical instrument

_____ 107. Playing baseball/softball

_____ 108. Playing basketball

_____ 109. Playing checkers

_____ 110. Playing chess

_____ 111. Playing darts

_____ 112. Playing football

_____ 113. Playing hide-and-go-seek

_____ 114. Playing horseshoes

_____ 115. Playing in a hideout/clubhouse

_____ 116. Playing in the sprinklers

_____ 117. Playing "king of the hill"

_____ 118. Playing marbles

_____ 119. Playing with a puppet

_____ 120. Playing with a wagon

_____ 121. Playing with babies/infants

_____ 122. Playing with dolls

_____ 123. Playing with jacks

_____ 124. Playing with toy cars

_____ 125. Playing with toy soldiers

_____ 126. Pool/billiards

_____ 127. Porch swings

_____ 128. Pottery making

_____ 129. Public speaking

_____ 130. Quilt making

_____ 131. Racketball

_____ 132. Rafting on (running) a river

_____ 133. Raising flowers

_____ 134. Reading

_____ 135. Receiving a massage (back rub)

_____ 136. Receiving an award, recognition

_____ 137. Recess during school

_____ 138. Riding a tricycle

_____ 139. Riding in a hot air balloon

_____ 140. Rock climbing

_____ 141. Rocking chairs

_____ 142. Rodeos

_____ 143. Sailing

_____ 144. Sand pile play

_____ 145. Sauna

_____ 146. Scuba diving

_____ 147. Sculpting/modeling in clay

_____ 148. Security (cuddle) blanket

_____ 149. Sewing

_____ 150. Shooting (rifle, pistol)

_____ 151. Singing

_____ 152. Sipping wine/cocktail

_____ 153. Sitting in front of a fire

_____ 154. Sitting in the backyard

_____ 155. Skateboarding/roller skating

_____ 156. Sky diving

_____ 157. Sleeping in late

_____ 158. Sleigh riding

_____ 159. Slippery slide

_____ 160. Smoking

_____ 161. Snowmobile riding

_____ 162. Snow ski/cross country ski

_____ 163. Snowball fight

_____ 164. Solving puzzles

_____ 165. Stage fright

_____ 166. Stuffed animals

_____ 167. Sunbathing

_____ 168. Surfing

_____ 169. Swimming

_____ 170. Swinging in a swing

_____ 171. Symphony concerts

_____ 172. Taking a nap

_____ 173. Television

_____ 174. Tennis

_____ 175. Thanksgiving day

_____ 176. The beach and ocean

_____ 177. The desert

_____ 178. The mountains

_____ 179. Too short for your age

_____ 180. Too tall for your age

_____ 181. Traffic jam

_____ 182. Train ride

_____ 183. Trampoline

_____ 184. Trap shooting

_____ 185. Traveling to a foreign country

_____ 186. Typing

_____ 187. Underweight (very skinny)

_____ 188. Very sick (ill)

_____ 189. Video games

_____ 190. Visiting relatives you like

_____ 191. Warm bath

_____ 192. Watching clouds drift by

_____ 193. Watching fireworks

_____ 194. Watching ice skating

about the unique background interests and values of patients. This information, much of which would not ordinarily be brought up in conversations, may subsequently be utilized by the therapist for individualizing treatment. The checklist is not intended as a substitute for the careful observation or skillful interviewing that Erickson repeatedly emphasized. It is simply a tool for expanding our knowledge base about patients and for identifying their self-perceptions.

When I use the checklist, I introduce it by telling patients that "hypnosis is most effective when it is individualized, taking into account your interests and life experiences. For example, suppose we were using mental imagery to help you to relax more deeply. We would not want to suggest that you imagine yourself skiing in the mountains if you dislike snow and have never been skiing. On the other hand, if you love the beach and find it very peaceful, it will probably be much more pleasant for you to imagine yourself at the beach." It is further explained, "The checklist will help me get better acquainted with you and to individualize hypnosis and treatment to your unique interests."

Such statements convey interest and respect to patients, as well as motivating them to complete the instrument. Patients are told, "The checklist will probably require 20–30 minutes to complete at home. Don't take more than that time. If you feel too puzzled about how to mark an individual item, just leave it blank." They are requested to bring the checklist to the next interview. In the next session, the checklist provides an opportunity and stimulus for briefly discussing a wide variety of topics which therapists seldom talk about with their patients. Subsequently, the instrument may be more thoroughly studied as part of the process of treatment planning.

I have now used the checklist with approximately 150 patients and in the training of more than 250 therapists. The checklist identifies over 200 life experiences and interests. In a space beside each item, clients give a rating on a 1 to 7 scale indicating if they like or enjoy the experience (past or present), feel neutral about it, or dislike the activity. They leave the item blank if it is not in their background of experience.

It cannot be overstressed that therapy should be individually prescribed, with individual methods being used according to their indications and contraindications (Hammond & Stanfield, 1977). As with any method in therapy, the author does not routinely use the checklist with all patients.

Times when the checklist will be less appropriate or contraindicated include: 1) in initial work with patients in crisis or with urgent problems, such as suicidal individuals or women with hyperemesis gravidarum; 2) when brief, highly focused hypnotic work is anticipated (e.g., with smoking, nailbiting, and direct symptom removal); 3) with patients who are very physically weak or ill (e.g., cancer and stroke patients, and some medical ward patients), for whom the checklist would prove a physical burden; 4) with patients with a very low frustration tolerance (e.g., manic, immature or impulsive patients, or court referrals) who may be overtly resistant or cannot thoughtfully complete tests and forms; 5) with severely disturbed patients who lack good reality contact, or who are very paranoid; 6) with culturally different or less educated patients who may have difficulty reading English.

In addition, the final section of the checklist will be of more limited value with patients extremely lacking in insight, who are not psychologically minded, and who will, therefore, have more difficulty realistically assessing their own needs and values.

On the other hand, use of the checklist may be indicated and particularly valuable: 1) with less verbal patients who do not reveal as much information; 2) with patients who are more difficult to read nonverbally; 3) when a moderate amount of hypnotic work or longer therapy is anticipated, so that the therapist has available a greater fund of information with which to avoid redundancy; 4) in complex cases that are more diffuse and focused on a large number of issues, where the therapist feels that extra information and careful treatment planning are particularly required; 5) with more compulsive patients and clients who express concern that they not be treated in some standardized manner.

When the checklist is used, it can rapidly provide an abundance of information for use in individualizing hypnotic induction and deepening techniques, therapeutic metaphors, and suggestions. For instance, a sure way to construct a truism that patients cannot deny is through knowing more about their life experiences. Thus, with someone who enjoys skiing, one can safely say, "There was a time when you didn't know how pleasurable and exciting skiing could be."

The checklist also provides information that may be beneficial in working with age regression, facilitating various hypnotic phenomena, creating symbolic imagery, and alerting the therapist to areas that may provoke unpleasant and negative reactions. The dislikes of the patients, particularly when they are things that would be good for them, may also be utilized in planning ordeals and paradoxical techniques (Haley, 1984).

A small number of negative life experiences were also included on the checklist, such as the death of a pet, feeling awkward on dates, being too short for your age, having a broken arm, or having a good friend move away. Such items are included because, despite their unpleasantness, these are experiences the patient successfully survived and mastered. Anesthesia and inpatient surgical experiences are also included on the checklist because negative anesthesia experiences are sometimes a source of resistance to hypnosis, and comments made during surgery may continue to be an unconscious source of influence (Cheek, 1959; Cheek & LeCron, 1968; Erickson, 1963).

Induction and Deepening

Patient interests can be used to internally fixate attention for purposes of trance induction and deepening. The checklist contains many items with imagery possibilities, such as being in the mountains, the symphony, a warm bath, watching clouds drift by, swimming, and sitting in front of a fire. How often does the reader utilize imagery of snow falling as an induction or deepening method? It has a hypnotic effect, but is such a common event that its potential may easily be overlooked. However, individualization is essential because some individuals strongly dislike snow or live in geographic regions where they rarely see snow. Therapists can be more creative and varied in technique after learning more about patient interests from a completed copy of the checklist.

Facilitating Hypnotic Phenomena

I also use background experiences identified by the checklist in facilitating various hypnotic phenomena. Several examples provide illustration. When a patient indicates an enjoyment of being outside in a thick fog, this type of experience can be used to facilitate disorientation preliminary to age regression, age progression, or depersonalization. One patient appreciated aquariums, so as an induction he visualized fish swimming in an aquarium. To facilitate arm levitation, I then suggested the imagery of seeing and feeling as if his hand were in the water, with bubbles floating up under the palm, while he sensed the hand buoyantly floating up.

An interest in doodling has been utilized to produce automatic writing, and could also be used to facilitate hypnography. Background experiences in carving, snow sculpting, or sculpting and modeling in clay may alert the therapist to the option of using hypnoplasty as a technique (Sacerdote, 1972). Knowledge of early background experiences (e.g., bedtime stories, stuffed animals, pets) have been used in promoting age regressions. Learning about childhood areas of competency and enjoyment also helps to target resources (e.g., spontaneity, confidence, security) that may be accessed for the patient through age regression.

Depending on the interests identified by the patient on the checklist, I may discuss the time distortion that takes place when absorbed in such activities as a video game, jogging, or painting. On the other hand, one may point out how time drags when one waits for a slow golf party, sits through a dull sermon, or is at a standstill in a traffic jam.

Applications of enjoyable experiences for use in dissociation and for facilitating ideosensory phenomena are readily apparent. Even suggestions for amnesia can utilize unique client experiences or interests. For instance, one can talk about the experience of falling asleep while listening to someone read you a bedtime story. With a patient who enjoys cooking, one may cite the example of reading a recipe and just a few moments later realizing you have forgotten the ingredients or amounts to be used. When formulating suggestions for automaticity and learning to trust the unconscious mind, I will often use client interests from the checklist such as, knitting, painting, playing a musical instrument, or various sports.

Symbolic and Projective Techniques

The checklist also helps me identify options to be used in symbolic imagery techniques. A patient who enjoys hiking may struggle up a mountain, overcoming obstacles on the climb, either in imagery, or with actual assignments like those Erickson used with Squaw Peak. A patient who had done snow sculpting was instructed to visualize making a snow sculpture symbolizing something in his life (e.g., fear, feelings of inadequacy, grief), and then, to watch it melt away in the early spring sun. Another patient who enjoys trap-shooting visualized shooting clay pigeons that were defined as symbolizing something he wanted to get rid of (anger).

Constructing Metaphors

Metaphors are a valuable Ericksonian technique, especially for bypassing resistance. However, metaphors are more impactful when they are relevant to the life experiences of the patient. Unfortunately, some therapists construct stories that have as little relevance to the background of the patient as "canned" metaphors that are identically used with each patient. However, spending a few minutes studying background information contained in the checklist often provides a stimulus for creatively preparing a metaphor that has personal meaning to the patient.

Some examples will provide illustration. In treating a patient with a sexual dysfunction who is kinesthetically responsive and also enjoys swimming, I use a metaphor of swimming. The sensory awareness of the experience is cited, interspersing ideas about stroking, buoyancy, stimulation, pressure, being playful, floating along peacefully, "going down" into the water, and absorbing oneself in the pleasure of each moment of the experience.

On the other hand, in working with the same problem in a patient who enjoys attending the symphony (and for whom auditory responsiveness is a hypnotic talent), we can focus on becoming deeply absorbed in the music rather than letting one's mind wander.

If a patient enjoys dining out, we may discuss the process of speaking up and placing one's own order without expecting one's partner to read your mind and know what you are in the mood for that night. We may then continue by discussing how one can savor each bite, being aware of the texture, the smell, the taste, and how nice it is to take time to enjoy it.

When working with a patient who spends considerable time watching television, there are many concepts that may be elaborated metaphorically and with wordplay: channel your attention; channel your energies; channels for the past, present and future; changing programs and reprogramming; static and interference; fine tuning. I might discuss the concept of the television trance, and how "we can tune out other things that right then we don't want to be attuned to. And when we are absorbed in the present, experience of the story, we channel our attention away from the day's tensions and tend to attend to the enjoyment of this experience and its feelings. And sometimes we get so tired of a black and white program, and we realize that life is so much more than black and white, that there are shades and colors that are missing. And things can look so different, so much richer, and the perspective can be so different when we put the color back in, to life."

Consider for a few moments the metaphoric possibilities of just a few items from the checklist: climbing a mountain; gardening; scuba diving (and discovering the mysteries beneath the sea); playing chess; bodybuilding; riding in a hot air balloon; cooking; gambling or card playing; a train ride; a jigsaw puzzle; fishing; hunting; being in a stage play; the mending of a broken arm or leg; hang gliding; playing football; learning to ride a bike, ski, golf, swim, water ski, or dance; the process of creating something through carving, sculpting or painting. As one can see, a thorough checklist of interests can become a stimulus for therapist creativity.

Utilizing Personality, Needs, and Values

In addition to assessing interests, Erickson also took into account personality styles, needs, cognitive patterns and the mental sets of the patient as he formulated treatment strategies and hypnotic suggestions. (For examples, see Rosen, 1982, pp. 149-150; Erickson & Rossi, 1981, p. 181; Rossi, 1980, Vol. 4, pp. 321-327). Therefore, in a final section of the checklist (see p. 122), patients are asked to rank order the importance of various needs and values.

In this section, phrased for the patient in everyday language, the client prioritizes the following needs: safety or security; achievement and challenge; perfection; compulsiveness (order, structure, organization); fun or playfulness; variety and stimulation (excitement); dependency and deference; independence or autonomy (freedom); affiliation (to make a good impression, to please and be liked); to be in control; to be loved; exhibition (to be seen and heard, entertain or amuse others); nurturance (to nurture and take care of others); dominance or to be "one-up" (influence or lead others); altruism

Needs, Values & Priorities

Please rank order the following needs according to their importance to you. Rank the most important as number 1 and the least important as 16. Please rank all 16 items.

_____ 1. To accomplish difficult things, excel and achieve.

_____ 2. For safety, security, stability, and to avoid risk.

_____ 3. To make a good impression, please, and be liked by others.

_____ 4. For order, structure, neatness, and to have things organized.

_____ 5. To be in control.

_____ 6. For perfection or to be the best.

_____ 7. To have fun (for playfulness).

_____ 8. To be loved.

_____ 9. To be seen and heard, entertain or amuse others.

_____ 10. To be guided, conform to custom, and follow guidelines.

_____ 11. To nurture, support, comfort and take care of others.

_____ 12. To have freedom to "do you own thing," and be independent.

_____ 13. To influence or lead others.

_____ 14. For variety and stimulation.

_____ 15. To be useful and of service.

_____ 16. To overcome obstacles, difficulties and weakness.

(Circle) Do you give more priority to:
    A. Your heart and feelings; or
    B. To your mind and reasoning.

(Circle) When learning something new, do you:
    A. Tend to critically judge and evaluate it while you are learning it; or
    B. Tend to accept it now and evaluate it later.

(Circle) Do you tend to be more critical of:
    A. Yourself.
    B. Others.
    C. Very critical of self and others.

(Circle) Does your thinking or daydreaming focus more on:
    A. The past.   B. The present.   C. The future.

(Circle) Do you tend to:
    A. Magnify, enlarge or exaggerate problems, or
    B. Minimize, de-emphasize and play down problems.

(to be useful and of service); and counteraction (to overcome obstacles, difficulties and weakness).

It is important to remember that accurate assessment of patient needs and values requires careful observation and skillful interviewing. Information in the checklist should be regarded as simply one more source of information. Patient self-perceptions may lack objectivity and must be weighed along with those of the therapist and the spouse. At the same time, patient perceptions can be valuable because as therapists we also can be quite subjective and at times engage in inaccurate "mind reading" from minimal cues.

As part of the assessment, I ask five other questions (in the final section of the checklist) which have patients categorize some of their cognitive sets. For instance, following the model of Spiegel and Spiegel (1978), does the patient emphasize emotions and feelings or the mind and reasoning? With patients who give priority to their heart, the therapist can stir feelings and appeal to emotions in formulating hypnotic suggestions. In treating a patient who emphasizes reasoning, the therapist can stress explanations, cite goals and rationales, and appeal to their intellectual curiosity.

Modifying diagnostic suggestions made in workshops by Jeffrey Zeig, several other items were added. One item seeks to determine if the patient tends to critically judge and evaluate things now, or is the type of person who suspends critical judgment and accepts things for now, evaluating them later. Phrased another way, is the patient more critical and objective, or more trusting and subjective?

Another question identifies the time orientation of the patient. Does the patient focus fantasies and thought more on the past, present, or future? A more present-oriented patient may enjoy a focus on the current experience in trance. In contrast, a past-oriented patient may like age regression work, which can focus on the positive past as well as negative experiences. When working with future-oriented patients, the therapist may focus on goals, planning, building expectancy and looking forward to things.

Another question seeks to determine whether the patient is intrapunitive, extrapunitive, or what we might call a "pathologist." Is the patient more self-critical, critical of others, or is he or she critical of everyone (self and others)? A different item asks patients to evaluate if they tend to be catastrophizers who magnify and exaggerate problems, or minimizers who deemphasize problems. When the patient's preexisting cognitive set is to exaggerate problems, the therapist can utilize the patient's own language in the phrasing of posthypnotic suggestions. For example, one may use words like "always," "never," "very," and "extremely," as modifiers in phrasing suggestions.

The final section of the checklist compiles information which is more complex in nature, requiring careful study and evaluation. As an example, consider the forethought required to individualize a hypnotic strategy and suggestions for a patient who: 1) is intrapunitive; 2) has strong dependency needs to conform and be guided; 3) has relatively high needs for safety and to be loved; 4) likes order and structure; 5) is past-oriented; 6) emphasizes his heart and feelings; and 7) tends to accept new things now and evaluate them later.

Contrast this with a different patient who: 1) likes to be dominant and one-up; 2) is perfectionistic and likes to be the best; 3) also expresses relatively high needs to be seen and heard, influence and lead, and be independent; 4) is extrapunitive; 5) is future-oriented; 6) emphasizes reason over emotion; and 7) tends to critically judge and evaluate things as they are presented.

Conclusion

In recent years many myths have been perpetuated about the therapeutic style of Milton Erickson (Hammond, 1984). One of those myths is that he encouraged therapists to simply spontaneously trust the wisdom of the unconscious. Erickson learned to trust his unconscious mind through decades of compulsive preparation in which he laboriously wrote out suggestions and metaphors ahead of time. He frequently spent many hours of careful planning of treatment for a patient. If we hope to emulate Erickson's skill, we must be willing to follow his model of disciplined preparation and not rationalize impulsive and sloppy clinical work as being spontaneous and "trusting the unconscious." If we lack Erickson's creativity, perhaps it is because we lack his dedication to thoughtful treatment planning.

The *Checklist for Utilizing Life Experiences, Interests and Values* is a clinical tool that was stimulated by Erickson's approach. It compiles information about the likes, dislikes and life experiences of patients. It also allows patients an opportunity to rate their own perceptions of their personality needs and mental sets.

Despite the inaccuracies of self-perceptions, it is valuable to consider patient perceptions and not rely solely on our own inferences as therapists. However, the reliability and consistency of patient response and the validity of the self-ratings of personality needs and cognitive sets should be established. For example, a study could compare spouse ratings of partner personality needs and mental sets. Other studies of concurrent validity need to be done to determine if self-ratings of personality needs correlate with established scales (e.g., from the Minnesota Multiphasic Personality Inventory, California Psychological Inventory, Personal Orientation Inventory) measuring similar constructs. As one example, does a self-rating of the strength of the need to create a good impression correlate significantly with the Good Impression Scale of the California Psychological Inventory?

The checklist has been a stimulus for both individualization and creativity. In a minimal amount of time it provides the author with an abundance of information, some of which may be readily used in tailoring inductions, deepening techniques and suggestions to the patient. However, full utilization of the compiled information requires spending at least a few minutes of the interview reviewing the checklist and encouraging patients to elaborate their answers. Afterwards, checklist responses should be thoughtfully studied as part of treatment planning. A time investment is required to construct new metaphors, consider unique hypnotic talents and skills, and individualize suggestions to the interests, needs and cognitive sets of the patient. However, perhaps one of Erickson's most important legacies and examples to us was that he was willing to thoughtfully take that kind of time, both for the patient and as an investment in his own growth.

References

CHEEK, D. B. (1959). Unconscious perception of meaningful sounds during surgical anesthesia as revealed under hypnosis. *American Journal of Clinical Hypnosis, 1*, 101–113.

CHEEK, D. B. & LeCRON, L. M. (1968). *Clinical hypnotherapy.* New York: Grune & Stratton.

ERICKSON, M. H. (1963). Chemo-anesthesia in relation to hearing and memory. *American Journal of Clinical Hypnosis, 6*, 31–36.

ERICKSON, M. H. & ROSSI, E. L. (1976). *Hypnotic realities.* New York: Irvington.

ERICKSON, M. H. & ROSSI, E. L. (1979). *Hypnotherapy: An exploratory casebook.* New York: Irvington.

ERICKSON, M. H. & ROSSI, E. L. (1981). *Experiencing hypnosis.* New York: Irvington.

HALEY, J. (1973). *Uncommon therapy.* New York: W. W. Norton.

HALEY, J. (1984). *Ordeal therapy.* San Francisco: Jossey-Bass.

HAMMOND, D. C. (1984). Myths about Erickson & Ericksonian hypnosis. *American Journal of Clinical Hypnosis, 26*, 236–245.

HAMMOND, D. C. & STANFIELD, K. (1977). *Multidimensional psychotherapy.* Champaign, IL: Institute for Personality and Ability Testing.

HOLROYD, J. (1980). Hypnosis treatment for smoking: An evaluative review. *International Journal of Clinical & Experimental Hypnosis, 28*, 341–357.

LANKTON, S. & LANKTON, C. (1983). *The answer within: A clinical framework of Ericksonian hypnotherapy.* New York: Brunner/Mazel.

LIEBERMAN, M. A., YALOM, I. D., & MILES, M. B. (1973). *Encounter groups: First facts.* New York: Basic Books.

NULAND, W. & FIELD, P. B. (1970). Smoking & hypnosis: A systematic clinical approach. *International Journal of Clinical & Experimental Hypnosis, 18*, 290–306.

ROSEN, S. (Ed.). (1982). *My voice will go with you: The teaching tales of Milton H. Erickson.* New York: W. W. Norton.

ROSSI, E. L. (Ed.). (1980). *The collected papers of Milton H. Erickson on hypnosis. Vol. 1: The nature of hypnosis & suggestion; Vol. 2: Hypnotic alteration of sensory, perceptual & psychophysiological processes; Vol. 4: Innovative hypnotherapy*. New York: Irvington.

SACERDOTE, P. (1972). Some individualized hypnotherapeutic technics. *International Journal of Clinical & Experimental Hypnosis, 20*, 1-6.

SPIEGEL, H. & SPIEGEL, D. (1978). *Trance & treatment*. New York: Basic Books.

ZEIG, J. K. (1980). *A teaching seminar with Milton H. Erickson*. New York: Brunner/ Mazel.

Experiences with Milton Erickson: Personal Therapy, Supervision, and Cases Reported by Former Patients

Jeffrey K. Zeig, Ph.D.

This paper presents examples of Milton H. Erickson, M.D. conducting supervision and psychotherapy with the author. Also included are previously unpublished reports by Erickson's former patients. From these cases it can be seen that part of Erickson's indirect method was to present commonsense advice "one step removed." Moreover, Erickson used his perceptiveness and expertise to create predictions that were powerful interventions.

Introduction

Within the contexts of personal therapy and professional supervision, Milton H. Erickson, M.D. helped me develop into a more positive and effective person and therapist. In this essay, I will present some of my more mem-

Adapted from *Experiencing Milton H. Erickson* by Jeffrey K. Zeig, Brunner/Mazel, in press. Presented as the Keynote Address at the San Diego Conference on Hypnotic & Strategic Interventions, February 8, 1985, San Diego, California. Also presented as Keynote Address at the First German Congress for the Hypnosis and Hypnotherapy of Milton H. Erickson, October 1984, Munich, West Germany.

Address reprint requests to: Jeffrey K. Zeig, Ph.D., The Milton H. Erickson Foundation, Inc., 3606 North 24th Street, Phoenix, AZ 85016.

orable experiences with Dr. Erickson—experiences that portray him both as a person, and as a therapist. I will also relate experiences reported to me by Erickson's former patients and students. Too often Erickson is thought of as a brilliant technician. One of the purposes of these vignettes is to portray Erickson as I perceived him—a superb human being first, and a master therapist second.

Jay Haley (1982) remarked that hardly a day went by when he did not use something that he had learned from Erickson. In my case, the measure is . . . hardly an hour! There are several outstanding aspects of Erickson's method that account for my enthusiasm. These aspects will be apparent in each of the cases that follow. Erickson's approach to teaching, supervision, and therapy was based on common sense. He would often present a simple, commonsense remedy with sufficient drama to make his advice come alive. Also, he would individualize the delivery of his message so that the listener could more easily understand and respond to the instructions contained therein. Finally, Erickson would often mobilize responsiveness indirectly. For example, he would often couch his commonsense advice in an analogy or an anecdote. By this means Erickson could stay "one step removed," which will be seen to be an important ingredient in effective therapeutic communication.

Erickson's ability to individualize the delivery of his messages was based on his perceptiveness of minimal cues. He attended to the very things that people generally learn to ignore. For example, human beings often delete aspects of sensory experience—steady state information in particular. The human perceptual system is a great "mismatch detector" and notices what is wrong in a given situation. In contrast, Erickson trained himself to attend to what is *right*, to pick up on the minimal cues that depict a patient's strengths. He knew that it is easier to promote change by building upon what patients do right rather than by analyzing what they did wrong.

I do not believe there was anything exceptionally profound about Erickson's advice. But as will be seen, his *approach* was profound in that he consistently made use of the obvious. Unfortunately, many therapists are so absorbed in their dynamic formulations that they overlook the obvious. However, Erickson watched for the obvious thing and then presented it back to patients so that they could respond therapeutically in their own way.

Utilizing Contexts and Injunctions

A hallmark of Erickson's approach was his ability to utilize context. Manipulation of the context and/or the patient's response to context can create therapeutic change. Erickson looked for things in the immediate reality situation that could be used therapeutically, often setting up situations where people would spontaneously realize their previously unrecognized abilities to change (Zeig, 1980; Dammann, 1982). His therapy was not limited to interpersonal exchange and psychological archaeology. Erickson understood that change occurs in a context that includes effective communication, and that effective communication utilizes context.

Another aspect of Erickson's approach was that he was sensitively attuned to his environment. He seemed to be always working to influence, to have an effect on others. Perhaps he seemed so alert because he was extraordinarily aware of the injunctive aspect of communication.

Watzlawick (1985) discussed the fact that communication is both indicative and injunctive, that denotation and connotation are present in every communication. Communication is indicative in that facts are reported. The injunctive part of the communication is usually a more covert message that says, "Do something!" It is the injunctive aspect of communication that promotes change.

To illustrate what is meant by "indicative" and "injunctive," consider Erickson's early learning set induction. The surface indication is a story about how people learn the task of writing: "When you first learned to write the letters of the alphabet, it was an awfully difficult task. Did you dot the 't' and cross the 'i'? How many bumps are there in an 'n' and an 'm'?"

There is more to this communication than the indicative aspect. There are also numerous injunctions in these two sentences. The overall injunction is, "Go into a trance." Another injunction is, "This task (trance) will be difficult but you can eventually do it automatically." The patient is prodded to "be confused" by the reference to crossing the "i" and dotting the "t." Additionally, the patient is directed to remember things from the past. The last sentence, by changing from past to present tense, also tells the patient to "be absorbed in the memory."

It is not so much a therapist's words or data that promote change. Change comes when patients respond to the therapist's injunction, having heard what the therapist indirectly tells them to do. More than other communicators, Erickson was keenly alert to the command aspect of communication.

Context is also part of communication and can be used injunctively. An example of Erickson's use of context arose in one of my first visits to him. At that time, Erickson was not so well known in wider psychological circles. *Uncommon Therapy* (Haley, 1973), the book that put Erickson in the limelight had just been published.

After a few visits I decided to videotape Erickson and so I brought my friend Paul to Phoenix. Paul was skilled in the use of videotape equipment and we wanted to make videos of Erickson at work because so few existed.

We set up the equipment and recorded Erickson performing a remarkable induction using Paul as a subject. Erickson was working with a patient who had no experience with hypnosis; he directed his efforts toward increasing both Paul's responsiveness and his ability to develop various hypnotic phenomena.

Unfortunately, I didn't get to enjoy it again; the tape was flawed. Paul had forgotten to plug the microphone into the videodeck, so we had a silent tape. As you can see from my wording, I blamed Paul and was more than a bit perturbed at him. I was quite possessive of my time with Erickson. Here I was sharing that time and the video was unusable.

The three of us discussed the problem that evening and Erickson would not let me continue to blame Paul. He pointed out that I was equally responsible for the failure. I acknowledged his point. However, secretly, I knew that he was wrong. I told myself that even Milton Erickson could make a sophomoric mistake! He did not seem to realize that a precious videotape was irretrievably lost; the taping was useless. However, unbeknownst to me, Erickson was going to make use of that silent tape.

The next day, when Paul and I were in Erickson's office, Erickson said to me, "Put on that silent tape." Then he looked at Paul expectantly. At the time, Paul was seated in the patient's chair. Paul looked at the video briefly and then he spontaneously went into a trance. Erickson had used that silent videotape as an induction technique! A common induction technique is to get a patient to remember a previous hypnotic experience and then access it. When Paul saw the trance that he had been in the day before, he went into a new trance. It didn't matter to him that there was no sound on the tape. Paul was sensitive to the situation. He intuited Erickson's intent and responded accordingly.

I got busy and set up the equipment so that we could tape this day's induction. While still in a trance Paul got out of his chair, and with his right hand cataleptic against his side (he was right-handed) walked to the videotape equipment and checked the sound plug using only his left hand. He was oblivious both to his surroundings and to the fact that his right arm was cataleptic. After returning to his seat, Paul looked up at Erickson and mechanically said, "I would like you to teach me more things while I am in this state."

Erickson thought that Paul's catalepsy was a fine example of lateralized behavior. He then underscored that were it not for the silent tape, we would never have had this excellent learning experience.

This incident is but one example of how Erickson used context. He established Paul's trance by merely manipulating the reality situation and communicating "one step removed," thereby creating an injunction to which Paul responded. And, characteristically, he did it in a way that accentuated the positive: the "useless" videotape turned out to be valuable!

Incidentally, that second induction is one of the few times when I saw Erickson miss something. As it turned out, Paul was quite responsive to minimal cues. During the induction, Erickson looked to me and said something like, "I can't see exactly what is happening, but his blink reflex is altered." While Erickson was talking, Paul's eyes closed.

Later, Erickson asked me when and why Paul closed his eyes. I didn't know. Erickson explained that Paul closed his eyes at the reference to the altered blink reflex. But in viewing the videotape, Paul and I realized Erickson was wrong. Actually, when Erickson had said, "I can't see . . . ," Paul was so attuned to minimal cues that he took the message literally and quickly shut his eyes. Literalism as evidenced by pinpoint responsiveness to injunctions is often a characteristic of good subjects. Paul had heard "*I can't see*" as the injunction "*Eye can't see*," and responded precisely.

Here is another example of Erickson's use of context. I didn't have enough money to afford extensive training at that time in my career, and it was Erickson's style not to charge if patients or students couldn't affort it. He didn't charge me for his time and I wanted to give him a gift to express my appreciation.

Erickson loved wood carvings; he had a large collection of ironwood carvings made by the Seri Indians who live in the desert of southwest Mexico. So I gave Erickson a wood carving, one with an unfinished driftwood base. The top of the carving was a finished duck's head. When I presented the gift to Erickson, he looked at the driftwood and looked at me. He looked at the driftwood, and looked at me. He looked at the driftwood, and looked at me. Then he said, "Emerging."

Erickson seemed to thrive on finding new opportunities to create influence communication by using aspects of the environment. In addition to utilizing context, he also was renowned for his use of other forms of indirection.

Utilizing Indirection

A common aspect of Erickson's approach was his use of indirection. Although he could be quite direct, characteristically he was indirect. Paradoxically, indirection is often the most direct method to promote change.

One way Erickson was indirect was that he structured his stories to have effects on multiple levels. In a teaching situation, his stories were not only interesting examples of good psychotherapy, but often relevant on the psychological level.

For example, Paul and I and another student were in Phoenix to learn from Erickson. The three of us were vying for Erickson's attention, and of course he noticed. Erickson abruptly changed his train of thought and told us a story about a competitive fellow from the East who came to see him and wanted to go into a trance (see Rosen, 1982, p. 81, for a complete case description).

Erickson used an arm levitation technique and said, "Okay. Now see which hand rises fastest."

One of us asked whether the story was intended to make reference to the competition between us. Erickson acknowledged that he felt the competition. He also remarked, "I certainly did not want there to be any competition directed toward me." Thereby, he implied that the competition could be redirected.

And thus he commented and empathized indirectly. He did not often empathize in the Rogerian sense. He would not have said, "It seems that you are feeling a need to compete." Instead, his story spoke to the idea of competition, and to the idea of redirecting it.

When he told his anecdote, we had not yet recognized the feeling of competing, but we picked up on his cue. When we directly talked with him about the idea of competing, he was perfectly willing to discuss the situation openly. His style did not require that issues had to remain at an unconscious level.

Politeness was one reason he didn't bring up the idea of competition directly. He responded with the same level of experience with which he was being presented. Had we openly talked about competition, I think he would have, too. But he believed in the integrity of the unconscious and in being courteous to the unconscious mind. It seemed he followed the dictum: If things are expressed unconsciously, respond accordingly; if things are expressed consciously, discuss them directly.

Using Anecdotes to Make Things Memorable

Erickson's anecdotes made simple ideas come alive. Not only are concepts more memorable when presented in story form (Zeig, 1980), but anecdotes energize the therapeutic situation. I learned this from Erickson because he helped me change my own life with his stories.

In 1978 I moved to Phoenix. Occasionally I consulted Erickson about my own professional or personal difficulties. I once told him I was troubled by a nervous habit of self-consciously smiling at inappropriate times. In response, he told me a story about his hands. He said that as a child he smashed the forefinger of his right hand and damaged the nail. Thereafter, when he went to pick up something valuable, he would pick it up without using his forefinger. But if it were something *not* valuable, he would pick it up using his forefinger. Erickson told me that he had a female student who knew about this habit. Once, this woman handed him her diamond engagement ring. Erickson looked at the ring and from the corner of his eye saw the woman had flushed. Then he looked down at his hand and realized that he was holding the ring using his forefinger. In other words, the ring was not a real diamond and she knew it.

That was the essence of Erickson's advice to me. I left his office confused.

When I thought about it, I realized that his discussion of the diamond ring was analogically saying that my problem wasn't real. It wasn't a bona fide thing! I began to think about the etiology of my "problem," possibly because Erickson had talked about the etiology of his own. At any rate, the therapy worked. I quit smiling self-consciously.

Erickson's anecdotes helped me again and again. On one occasion, early in my training, I told Erickson I was afraid of trance. He asked why and I explained, "I don't know. Maybe I'm afraid of blacking out."

Erickson said that he would give me a few examples. He told me about a boy who went hunting with his father. Erickson said that the boy enjoyed deer hunting until the age of 16, when the father announced the son was old enough to go out on his own. The boy was given a gun and he shot a deer. His unexpected reaction was to tremble and go white.

Next Erickson told a story about a beauty contest. He said that the winner of the Miss America Pageant cries and trembles.

Then he talked about giving birth. He told of a woman who was afraid of delivery even though she realized that throughout history women easily accomplished the process. Subsequently, Erickson explained to me that I had been in and out of a trance during the session on the previous day.

I then told him I wanted "an anchor experience" so that I could understand how to use hypnosis. He told me two more stories.

The first was about a baseball player who missed the ball when he anchored himself. The second was about a medical student who repeated his first year of medical school seven times. When asked what the deltoids were, he would recite verbatim from page one of the textbook. He went back to page one because he needed to anchor himself.

Erickson then looked at me and said, "You want to be able to use hypnosis for various periods of time. You go in and out by letting it happen."

The effect of these stories was to produce an enhanced ability to utilize my hypnotic abilities; no longer was I afraid of an untoward reaction from hypnosis.

Anecdotes of this sort are easily interpretable. Basically Erickson was redefining my fear of blacking out and allowing me to accept that part of the initial process of learning may include unexpected emotions. In essence, this technique of redefinition allowed for a more positive interpretation of blacking out (i.e., similar feelings can occur after a triumph), and a more negative interpretation of the need for an anchor. But when one overanalyzes stories, often the gestalt is lost. The total is more than the sum of the parts.

Indirection Using Analogies

Once Erickson presented me with a bit of advice in the form of a rather nice analogy. Unfortunately, I have yet to completely follow the advice, but I have used the same analogy effectively with some of my patients.

I explained to Erickson that I had been working too hard and asked him for some assistance. He talked with me about his own life. He said that during the years he worked at Eloise Hospital in Michigan he regretted not taking enough vacations with his family.

Then he gave an example. "When a man sits down for a meal, he might want to have a cocktail. Then he could have an appetizer. After that, he might want to have a palate refresher. Then he might want to have a salad, and then there is the main course, which has meat and some kind of carbohydrate, and a vegetable. After that, there would be a dessert, and then there would be coffee or tea." Then Erickson looked up at me and said, "Man cannot live by protein alone."

Part of Erickson's mentality was to present ideas by getting one step removed from the situation. Being *one step removed* is the essence of indirection.

The advice I needed to hear was, "Don't work too hard." There wasn't really much more that he could say to me but, "Well, don't work so hard." But Erickson gave his advice in terms of an analogy that made the idea memorable and alive.

Indirection to Guide Associations

Anecdotes do not merely energize the therapy and make ideas memorable; they are also used to guide associations. Problems are often caused by preconscious associations. If problems are generated at the level of associations, it is at that level that they often can be best changed. Anecdotes can be used to help reassociate the patient's internal life. Merely talking about a situation is not necessarily therapeutic.

I remember how Erickson got me to stop smoking a pipe. I was an addicted pipe smoker, and he didn't approve of smoking. On some level, I must have approved. At the time, it fit my image of being "the young psychologist."

Erickson saw me smoking my pipe in his backyard. (I would not smoke inside his office.) When I came in for our session, he told me a long lighthearted, convoluted story about a friend of his who was a pipe smoker. As I remember it, this friend looked awkward smoking his pipe, and he also looked awkward putting tobacco into the pipe.

I remember thinking, "I've been smoking a pipe for years. I don't look awkward." Erickson continued to tell me how the friend looked awkward: He looked awkward when he tamped the tobacco down; he looked awkward when he lit up the tobacco; he looked awkward because he didn't know where to put his pipe; he looked awkward because he didn't know how to hold the pipe.

I swear this story went on for an hour. I never knew that there were so many

different ways that someone could look awkward. All the time I kept thinking to myself, "Why is he telling me this story? *I* don't look awkward."

Shortly after the session, I left Phoenix to drive back to San Francisco
where I lived.When I reached California, I said to myself, "I am not smoking anymore." I put away the pipe forever. I got rid of all my expensive pipes
and lighters.

I had responded to Erickson's injunction. I certainly didn't want to look
awkward in his eyes. Moreover, this technique was a pattern disruption; he
attached the idea of awkwardness to pipe smoking. Subsequently, smoking
a pipe just didn't seem appealing.

Direct Supervision

Erickson was an unusual supervisor whose instructions, like his therapy,
were based on one-step removed common sense. His technique as a supervisor was as unique as his technique as a therapist and teacher. Here are some
examples.

Case One

After Erickson retired from private practice, he referred a number of patients to me. One of these had a peculiar contamination phobia. Whenever
he saw white powder on anything he became phobic about that object forever and would avoid it, to the point where he was terrorizing his acquain-
tances and family. For example, he once saw white powder on the television,
and because he wouldn't touch it, his wife and daughters had to turn the television on and off and change the channels for him.

In the first session with this patient, I got a history and description of the
man's problem. Then I called Erickson and asked him for supervision. He
agreed to see me, and so I went to his home and told him about the patient
in elaborate detail. I asked how he would handle the problem. Erickson's advice was simple. He stoically said, "Send him to Canada." Then he added,
"As a matter of fact, send him to northern Canada."

Erickson told me this type of patient was possibly capable of becoming vio-
lent: He could get the idea that someone had intentionally put white powder
on an object to contaminate him.

Erickson didn't have anything more to say. I didn't accept the advice about
Canada because I didn't have any idea what he'd meant, but I was sufficiently
wary that I only worked with the patient for one more session. In essence,
I gave him a behavioral technique of pattern disruption and told him how
to apply it. Because of the man's particular dynamics, I wanted the man to

depend on himself rather than on my intervention. I told him not to contact me regardless of whether or not the therapy I suggested was successful. I left it all up to him.

Sometime after the therapy, I was musing about Erickson's advice. I finally got it. When Erickson initially gave me his advice about the case, I was too stunned by his brief, impassive response to immediately realize what he was talking about. Also, when you live in the Phoenix desert area, it is easy to forget about the weather in the northern latitudes. Erickson had been suggesting an *in vivo* desensitization! I believe that Erickson did not literally mean that I should send the man to Canada. Rather he was directing me to look for contexts in which the problem wouldn't exist. At the same time he was suggesting that I rely on my own resources, not his advice.

Case Two

Another case that Erickson referred to me was one in which he worked with four generations of a family: He had seen the grandfather, the father, the two sons, and the family of one of the sons. He referred the depressed wife of one of the sons. Erickson told me about the pattern of failure that existed in the men of the family, and he explained that the husband was rigid, aloof, and emotionally unexpressive. Part of the wife's depression was due to the fact that her husband was emotionally distant.

During the course of the treatment, I consulted Erickson a number of times. At one point, the woman was going to sell her business. I didn't think that this was a good idea and so I asked Erickson about it. He told me to tell her, "Keep the business because it sets a good example for the children." His advice was on target. Although he had seen the wife only once previously, he had ascertained her values. One of the primary things in her life was being a good model for her children.

With subsequent therapy, I helped the wife but I thought not enough. I discussed the situation with Erickson again. He responded with a story. It was an anecdote about the Seri Indians who made ironwood carvings. Erickson explained that the Seri Indians were poor and had only primitive tools. After a day of fishing, they might catch only one or two fish for the tribe. At night, they would walk out into the desert and sleep underneath the stars.

He explained that an anthropologist, who subsequently became a personal friend, visited the Seris. The man interested the Indians in fashioning wood carvings from the ironwood readily available in the Sonoran Desert. The Indians made ironwood carvings of the wild animals they knew. They used no models; the carvings were made from their own memory. They used primitive tools—ocean sand as sandpaper, shoe polish as dye.

The carvings became extremely popular and the Seri Indians became rich.

Now they were able to buy fishnets and pickup trucks. Erickson explained that they would throw their fishnets into the ocean and soon they would catch a lot of fish for the tribe. Then Erickson said, "And then they would take their pickup trucks and drive out into the desert and sleep underneath the stars."

That was Erickson's advice about this woman. Again, I had to do some processing to get the point, but the message became clear: Even though some people change their circumstances, they may not really change their fundamental attitudes or behaviors.

If Erickson had told me, "You know, some people don't change their fundamental behavior even when their circumstances change," I wouldn't have remembered it. He made his point memorable by weaving it into a dramatic, one-step removed vignette.

I also conducted some "family therapy" in this case, using a device I had learned from Erickson. He had told me about a technique he used to encourage communication in emotionally distant families. He would tell family members to take turns reading the Ann Landers column from the newspaper. They were to do this each night at the dinner table for one year. The *letters* were to be read, but the *replies* were to be saved until after some family discussion (with the stipulation, of course, that although much of her advice is sound, it may not necessarily be correct or the only solution or applicable to the family at that time. Erickson said if you read Ann Landers for a year, you have encountered the whole gamut of human problems.

I've used this technique on a number of occasions. It's an excellent way to push a family toward more contact and the discussion of moral issues.

Case Three

I had a difficult schizophrenic patient and I asked Erickson for supervision. Erickson asked if the patient liked music. When he found out the patient was musically inclined, he said, "Well, if the patient plays the piano, have him learn to play a song one note off." Because the patient played the guitar, I had him learn a song one fret off.

The advice was quite sensible because it was symbolic of the actions of schizophrenic patients; they live their lives just a bit off-key. But in order to play a song off-key, one has to learn it correctly first. I have used variations of this method often in my work with schizophrenic patients.

Case Four

Although I've already published one of my favorite cases of supervision (Zeig, 1980), I will provide some additional details here.

An attorney contacted Erickson about a case in which he believed hypnosis was being used improperly. It was a murder case in which the police used hypnosis on the witnesses. The defense attorney asked Erickson if he would testify in the case, but Erickson said that he was too old and suggested the attorney call me.

I told the defense attorney that I had never testified in a courtroom before, but I would be glad to render an opinion about whether or not the hypnosis was used properly. The attorney said that he would have to submit my credentials to the court before he could use me as an expert witness. The attorney told the court that I was trained by Milton Erickson, the world's foremost authority on hypnosis, and my credentials were accepted.

Subsequently, the prosecuting attorney contacted Erickson. Erickson had taught investigative hypnosis to special officers on the staff of the Phoenix police force. In fact, he may have trained the officer who conducted the hypnotic session in this particular case. Erickson told the prosecuting attorney that he couldn't testify because of his infirmity. So the prosecuting attorney asked if he would give a deposition. Erickson agreed.

When the prosecuting attorney submitted Erickson's credentials to the court, he noted, "As the defense has acknowledged that Milton Erickson is the foremost authority on hypnosis, we would like to have him render an opinion in this case." Of course, Erickson was accepted by the court.

So it was Erickson for the prosecution, and Zeig for the defense. Needless to say, I got a little nervous.

I asked Erickson why he had changed his mind and decided to testify, and he said, "You have got a few things to learn, haven't you?" and I said, "You bet."

Even though it was difficult for Erickson to travel, he rode in the police van to the station to view the videotape. In addition to wanting to instruct me, Erickson must have thought that the case was important.

As we talked, I told Erickson I was nervous about going to court, and asked him for some advice. He initiated the following story with the phrase, "Know the opposing attorney."

Erickson explained that he had once testified in a child custody case on behalf of the husband. He believed the wife was suffering from severe psychological problems and that the husband was the best person to have custody, since it was possible the wife would be abusive.

Erickson then went on to say that he had suspected the opposing attorney was a very thorough individual. He'd figured things would be difficult because the husband's attorney did not give him any information about the opposition. He explained that when the day came for him to give his testimony, the opposing attorney came well prepared; she had 14 typewritten pages of questions for Erickson. She opened with a challenging question: "Dr. Erickson, you say that you're an expert on psychiatry. Who is your authority?" Erickson responded, "I am my *own* authority." He knew that if he named someone, this well-prepared lawyer would begin to undermine his expertise by citing conflicting authorities.

The lawyer then asked, "Dr. Erickson, you say that you are an expert in psychiatry. What is psychiatry?" Erickson said that he provided the following response: "I can give you this example. Anyone who is an expert on American history would know something about Simon Girty, also called 'Dirty Girty.' Anyone who is not an expert on American history would not know about Simon Girty, also called 'Dirty Girty.' Any expert on American history should know about 'Simon Girty,' also called 'Dirty Girty.'"

Erickson explained that when he looked up at the judge, the judge was sitting with his head buried in his hands. The clerk of the court was underneath the table trying to find his pencil. The husband's lawyer was trying to suppress an uncontrollable laugh.

After Erickson gave that (seemingly irrelevant) analogy, the lawyer put aside her papers and said, "No further questions, Dr. Erickson." Then Erickson looked at me and said, "And the lawyer's name . . . was Gertie."

Erickson's anecdote was amusing and engaging, a delightful way to make a point. If Erickson had simply told me, "Don't be intimidated by this situation," the impact would have been minimal. But as a result of this one-step removed method of communication, it is now impossible for me to go into a courtroom without thinking of "Dirty Girty."

Later, Erickson talked about another technique he used successfully in the courtroom. He said that often the opposing attorney would build emotional momentum and then pose an impassioned question, the inanity of which was obscured by the emotion of the moment.

At this point, Erickson would act a bit dumb. He would say to the judge, "I am sorry. I missed that question. Would you please have the clerk read it back to me?" Erickson said that when the court clerk read the question back in a flat voice it lost all of its dramatic intensity, allowing the jury and everyone else in the court to see how stupid the question really was.

After the murder case was resolved when the defendant pleaded guilty, Erickson and I discussed our findings with each other. We agreed that the hypnosis had not been used improperly. In fact, Erickson said that because the officer had used a standardized technique, the hypnosis actually had little effect on the subject; few responses were actually elicited.

Predictions

To create powerful interventions, Erickson used his perceptiveness of minimal cues and his acquired knowledge of how the patient's social history was influential in determining present problems. I have seen patients of Erickson's who were surprised by the accuracy of his predictions.

Case One

One woman came to Erickson as a student. He had her write down the customary information that he requested of all new patients and students — present date, name, address, telephone, marital status, number of children (names and ages), occupation, education (including degrees and universities attended), age, birthdate, number of brothers and sisters (names and ages), and whether the person's formative years were spent in an urban or rural environment.

While this woman was writing, Erickson said to her, "You are European." She confirmed this but did not think very much of his observation. There is quite a difference between the script of someone who learned to write in Europe and that of someone who learned to write in the United States.

Then Erickson said, "You are probably southern European, either from Italy or Greece." She thought that was not unusually perceptive; her coloring indicated her background.

Then Erickson shifted into high gear. He said to her, "And you were fat when you were a child." The patient was floored. At the time of her visit she was quite thin. She asked Erickson how he knew. He explained that she held herself the way a fat person did.

Erickson's incisive intervention had a number of effects. He took control of the relationship and broke the patient out of any preconceived set that she might have attempted to establish. Moreover, he established his credibility as a diagnostician and observer. He meticulously trained himself to attend to minute details and use that information to predict sequences of behavior.

Case Two

One of Erickson's former patients consulted me after Erickson died. I asked her if she remembered any special experiences with Erickson. She said that during the initial interview, Erickson had looked up at her and said, "You were not your mother's favorite." She was a little shocked and replied affirmatively.

Erickson then said, "You were your grandmother's favorite, probably your maternal grandmother." Again he was right. The patient was surprised at his perceptiveness and impressed with his acumen. Again, Erickson made good use of his diligent self-training and attentiveness to minimal cues.

Comment

These are examples of Erickson as I knew him as a teacher and therapist. He was quite consistent as a communicator, both professionally and personally; he was interested in having the maximum effect on the people with whom he was talking. To achieve these ends, he often tailored subtle techniques to guide associations so that to their own credit patients could discover their own resources and surmount learned limitations. One aspect of his method was to determine the commonsense advice needed by his patient and then present it one step removed, thereby increasing patient-based therapeutic responses.

References

DAMMANN, C. A. (1982). Family therapy: Erickson's contribution. In J. K. Zeig (Ed.), *Ericksonian approaches to hypnosis and psychotherapy* (pp. 193–200). New York: Brunner/Mazel.

HALEY, J. (1973). *Uncommon therapy: Psychiatric techniques of Milton H. Erickson, M.D.* New York: Norton.

HALEY, J. (1982). The contribution to therapy of Milton H. Erickson, M.D. In J. K. Zeig (Ed.), *Ericksonian approaches to hypnosis and psychotherapy* (pp. 5–25). New York: Brunner/Mazel.

ROSEN, S. (1982). *My voice will go with you: The teaching tales of Milton Erickson.* New York: Norton.

WATZLAWICK, P. (1985). Hypnotherapy without trance. In J. K. Zeig (Ed.), *Ericksonian psychotherapy, Vol. I: Structures.* New York: Brunner/Mazel.

ZEIG, J. K. (Ed.). (1980). *A teaching seminar with Milton H. Erickson.* New York: Brunner/Mazel.

Book Reviews

CLINICAL HYPNOSIS: A MULTIDISCIPLINARY APPROACH by William C. Wester, II and Alexander H. Smith. *Philadelphia: Lippincott, 1984, 660 pages, $35.00, hardbound.*

The number of new books on hypnosis and hypnotherapeutic approaches has increased dramatically in the last few years, with new offerings reaching the public each month. The vast majority to date have been theoretical or research-oriented in nature, with little direct clinical application and therefore lacking relevance for practitioners. However, that situation is beginning to change as hypnosis gains respectability as a therapeutic modality. There have been a few practitioner-oriented books to reach the market recently, generally on specific clinical problems. The danger now is that hypnosis will be applied indiscriminately to every conceivable client concern by minimally trained and supervised individuals with little or no consideration of its appropriate usage in light of theory and research. In particular, it is often difficult to determine if positive therapeutic outcome is the result of hypnosis *per se* or of some other therapist, client or situation variable. Likewise, therapists may not always consider whether hypnosis is theoretically indicated and, if so, how it is employed, but may use it because clients request or demand it. If such practices become widespread, hypnosis may again undergo one of the periodic extinctions that have plagued its history.

The present edited book neatly avoids either extreme of the irrelevantly theoretical or the mindlessly practical, and is an excellent amalgam of theory, research, and practice. It contains 29 chapters written by some of the foremost authorities in the field, many of whom are experts on the topics on which they write. For example, it includes Daniel Araoz on hypnotherapy for sexual dysfuncitons, Martin Orne on forensic hypnosis, William Kroger on hypnotherapy and behavior modification, and Erika Fromm on hypnoanalysis. Also included are other authors who are not as obviously identified with their topics. However, both groups of chapters are quite well done.

The book is organized into five units, with several chapters in each unit. Unit One, *Orientation to the practice of hypnosis*, contains chapters on historical development, preparing the patient, using the patient's breathing rhythm, induction and deepening techniques, hypnotic phenomena, and susceptibility tests. Unit Two, *Theoretical and experimental foundations for the practitioner*, contains chapters on sources of efficacy in the hypnotic relationship, hypnotherapy and behavior modification, Ericksonian hypnosis, hypnoanalysis, and cognitive-experiential hypnosis. Unit Three, *Hypnotic applications in medicine, psychology, and dentistry*, includes chapters on hypnosis with children, hypnosis in surgery, pain control, habit disorders, family therapy, dentistry, and miscellaneous medical conditions. Unit Four, *Use of hypnosis with psychopathological states*, includes hypnosis in psychiatry for depression, anxiety, somatic disorders, sexual dysfunctions, and with severely disturbed patients. Unit Five, *Distinctive innovations for the practitioner*, includes chapters on forensic hypnosis, and hypnosis in management training, sports, education and school psychology, and religion. Truly, one can hardly conceive of wider applications! There is something here for everyone!

The individual chapters are generally well written and thorough. The editors seem to have provided each author with a chapter guideline to follow. The chapters follow a similar basic pattern and the book thus appears coherent and with less overlap among chapters than is often the case with edited books. In each chapter, basic theory is usually set forth first, followed by (or integrated with) relevant research findings, and concluding with more or less detailed technique guidelines. These detailed therapeutic suggestions are among the most valuable aspects of the book and practitioners will gain much from reading and studying them. Especially valuable is the inclusion of typescripts of actual hypnotherapeutic inductions and/or routines, often found in appendices which follow many of the chapters. Indeed these appendices are of such value and quality that one wonders why all the technique chapters (at least) do not contain them. In at least one instance, the appendix is considerably longer than its chapter! The techniques follow logically from the theory and research which precede them. The only disappointment is that in a few cases the chapters are really too brief to do justice to the topic and readers are only titillated.

Interestingly, considering that both authors are counseling psychologists, the book is permeated with a subtle psychoanalytic flavor, even in some of the chapters which are not obviously analytic in nature. The chapter authors also make clear, either implicitly in their case examples and discussion of techniques or explicitly in their recommendations, that hypnosis is an adjunctive technique to be used in the context of ongoing therapy and in conjunction with other therapeutic interventions and is not a solo cure.

The major difficulty we had with the book was its unusual and often obscure organization. This was true both for the unit organization and the chapter organization. For example, Unit Three, which includes applications in psychology, does not include psychopathology, while the latter includes anxiety and sexual dysfunctioning, which do not appear particularly pathological. Medicine, psychology, and dentistry are lumped together as if they had something in common, while hypnosis in psychiatry is given a separate chapter even though the specific treatment applications include disorders covered in more detail in other chapters. Basic theoretical information about hypnosis is spread throughout several chapters in both units One and Two, and to some extent in other chapters as well. The editors seemingly could not decide whether to organize by type of problem or by type of setting. By including both, they have unfortunately exacerbated what otherwise might have been minimal conceptual overlap in chapter material. The result is that this is not a book that should be read by those who wish to familiarize themselves with fundamental information about hypnosis: It is for those professionals with some rudimentary knowledge about hypnosis who wish to learn more theory and some practical applications.

These are minor flaws in an otherwise excellent effort, however. Wester and Smith have done a thorough job of presenting a large amount of material covering very diverse applications and settings. Their book will be especially valuable to practitioners who have a smattering of knowledge in hypnosis and who wish to extend the range of their therapeutic interventions into an exciting field. It has been noted that many professionals who take an introductory course in hypnosis rarely use it subsequently. This book should go a long way towards rectifying that situation.

E. Thomas Dowd, Ed.D.,
Professor, Counseling Psychology,
University of Nebraska

James M. Healy, Ph.D.,
private practice,
Tallahassee, Florida

HEALING IN HYPNOSIS BY MILTON H. ERICKSON **edited by Ernest L. Rossi, Margaret O. Ryan and Florence A. Sharp.** *New York: Irvington, 1983, 310 pages, $39.50, hardbound with audio cassette.*

The goal of this volume is to collect and preserve Milton Erickson's teachings in hypnosis, human development and hypnotherapy. It was prepared for publication after Erickson's death by editors Rossi and Ryan from editor Sharp's collection of transcripts of Erickson's teaching seminars and lectures. It includes three presentations taped between 1961 and 1965, a biographical sketch of Erickson, and a collection of photographs of Erickson from childhood until just before his death in 1980.

Unlike some thinkers whose work is more accessible through writings of their colleagues, Milton Erickson is one of the best writers on Erickson. He employs a straightforward narrative style and expresses complex ideas in simple language. Senior editor Ernest Rossi has been a major force in the collection and publication of Erickson's work, with the four-volume *Collected Papers of Milton H. Erickson* previously to his credit. The *Collected Papers* offer a comprehensive gathering of Erickson's scholarly investigations and reports. In this volume Erickson's ideas are presented in a more casual teaching format, a relatively consolidated and accessible form.

The focus of the book is Erickson's thinking about the interpersonal aspects of hypnosis. It articulates his essential ideas about human nature, such as his understanding of the unconscious as a repository of untapped skills and resources. It describes the techniques which derive from these understandings, including utilization of the client's behaviors, use of the double bind, etc. And it details hypnotherapeutic solutions to a variety of clinical problems.

It is a little odd to read these "preserved" teachings from just two decades ago. Erickson persuasively elaborates ideas that were revolutionary at the time, charging therapists with responsibility for creating learning experiences that utilize all of their clients' behaviors, including resistance. In the time since, Erickson's many influential colleagues and students have promulgated his ideas far beyond the society of hypnotists whom he identifies as his audience for these presentations. Family therapy, especially, has embraced Erickson's ideas about directive, strategic intervention, and a new generation of therapists will find his ideas familiar and congenial.

Today the situation has reversed from one in which hypnotists take an interest in Erickson to one in which psychotherapists intrigued by Erickson's ideas begin to investigate hypnosis. In this new context Erickson's points of emphasis are not entirely congruent with his audience's learning needs. His allusions to hypnotic technique will be inadequate for psychotherapists not trained in hypnosis to fully and practically understand his work. While this book provides an excellent grounding in the principles of Ericksonian psychotherapy, practitioners will need to develop hypnotic skills elsewhere before they can make use of the many valuable clinical suggestions included here.

I think the editors have done an excellent job of accomplishing precisely the task they set themselves. Throughout the book they retain the casual and spontaneous quality of Erickson's teaching, transcribing the anecdotes, case descriptions and audience demonstrations that were Erickson's vehicle for expressing his ideas.

They have organized the book in a way that shows Erickson's work to advantage, employing structure to provide emphasis and restraining editorial additions. For example, emphasis on the importance of Erickson's thinking about interpersonal context in hypnosis is achieved simply by having the book begin and end with this material.

Each presentation is divided into short sections set off by content heads which are keyed to a thorough index. This organization facilitates its use as a clinical reference, and the volume is sufficiently rich in clinical detail to warrant such use.

In his introduction Rossi develops a teaching tale about Milton Erickson as "the wounded healer," interwoven with a chronology of Erickson's personal and professional development. He uses key vicissitudes in Erickson's life to introduce important principles of his work — for example, Erickson's personal discovery of ideomotor behavior during his recovery from polio at age 17, or the way his own perceptual limitations led him to understand human perception as relative and to take an interest in learning strategies that employ individual idiosyncratic strengths and limitations.

The pictures that close the book reveal a youthfully vigorous Erickson who may surprise those whose previous exposure to him has been limited to videotapes filmed during his later years of diminished health and vitality. The book is also accompanied by an audiotape reproducing the lecture transcribed in Part One. It is of excellent quality, providing readers an introduction to Erickson's unique voice, and interesting for the slightly different emphasis given the material in the written and spoken versions.

The editors intend this as the first in a series of volumes which will collect representative teachings from different eras of Erickson's practice. The historical perspective such a series promises is intriguing, and I look forward to publication of successive volumes.

Jodie Wigren, MSW
Boston, Massachusetts

MY VOICE WILL GO WITH YOU, THE TEACHING TALES OF MILTON H. ERICKSON edited and with commentary by Sidney Rosen. *New York: Norton, 1982, 256 pages, $16.95, clothbound.*

At first glance this seems an easy book: It is not very long, the structure is straightforward, the language is simple. Readers, therefore, may be surprised to discover its complexity. It was only when I read this book *with care* that I discovered Dr. Erickson's active presence in the reveries which were stimulated by reading each tale. *Skimming* through this book, however, and looking for the voice of Milton Erickson, I did not seem to find it. This is one of those rare books that is simple and yet which deserves an attentive reader.

The tales gathered in this book illustrate a teaching style which Erickson used increasingly in his later years. Like all good teachers, Erickson didn't just teach; he provoked learning. What was unique about Erickson was the degree to which he was willing to forgo explicit explanation about the intent of his teaching. He thus required each learner to grapple with the material he presented in a personal way. *My Voice Will Go With You* succeeds in creating an "Ericksonian" learning experience. The reader who allows time to savor and ruminate over each tale will learn something that is useful in an idiosyncratic way. It is clear that this is what Erickson intended.

Sidney Rosen accepts a number of challenges in undertaking to write a book on Erickson's teaching tales. The first is simply the difficulty of conveying the spoken word in print. Another is providing enough explanation to illuminate Erickson's work without overshadowing it. A third is constructing a book that will itself work as the teaching tale the title of this book encourages readers to expect.

The spoken word and the printed word are substantially different forms. One of the pleasures of Erickson's writing is his ability to convey his ideas simply and straightforwardly. In his spoken work he uses language very differently; rapport is established with subtle, nonverbal communications, meaning is conveyed by the pace, tone and manner of delivery, while the words themselves may hold little sense. Since these crucial facets of spoken communication cannot be readily conveyed in print, the printed translation risks losing both the power and the meaning of the spoken original.

However, in rendering these tales Rosen has made poetic use of the printed word. He uses italics to suggest vocal inflections. He has refrained from correcting Erickson's ingeniously incorrect grammar. He retains Erickson's unannounced shifts in persona of both speaker and subject to recreate the surprise and wonder which Erickson evoked so effectively. He has thus produced a book of written tales that conveys the hypnotic quality of Milton Erickson's teaching. That is an impressive accomplishment.

The comments with which Rosen frames Erickson's stories are equally successful. Erickson's mastery is like that of a ballet dancer: His artistry and technical accomplishment reveal themselves in his ability to perform difficult maneuvers simply, without extraneous movement. Without some explanation, a naive reader might easily miss much of the careful intention behind Erickson's simple moves.

But there are hazards in attempting to explicate Erickson's work. Sometimes Erickson's students become so excited by the intricacies they see embedded in his work that they overwhelm the work itself with eager explanations. Further, since Erickson so frequently expressed himself indirectly, a certain modesty is required in conjecturing as to his intent.

Rosen has more authority than most in speaking to Erickson's intent. A longtime colleague, he was Erickson's personal choice as editor of this volume. He has organized Erickson's tales into thematic chapters. His introductions to chapters and individual tales provide a context for listening to the teachings in the tales. At the end of most tales he briefly comments on Erickson's intent and draws our attention to certain technical subtleties we might otherwise overlook. The warm and personal style of Rosen's writing provides a complementary frame for Erickson's stories. Further, he has wisely refrained from attempting to elucidate every aspect of Erickson's technique, giving the reader the gift of relatively direct access to the teaching tales.

The tales themselves are a delight. People often ask, "Where do you get your stories?" From life, Erickson's tales suggest, as he tells of his family and others for whom he has cared. These are not dramatic stories, filled with intriguing twists of plot, nor are they moralistic in the tradition, for example, of Aesop's Fables. They intrigue with their homeliness and pique our curiosity with the odd bits of information Erickson garnered in a lifetime of extraordinarily acute observation of ordinary phenomena. Practitioners will find here both specific additions to their personal repertoires of teaching tales and a model for telling these stories.

Although the book itself works marvelously as a teaching tale, I suspect that readers new to Erickson will be puzzled and perhaps disappointed by precisely this aspect of the work. The inviting title and deceptive simplicity of the book make it a first choice for many who wish to begin learning about Milton Erickson. However, while it provides a rich learning experience, it teaches *about* Milton Erickson in a typically Ericksonian way — that is, indirectly and by example. Informal discussions with colleagues suggest that my own initial ambivalence about this is not unusual.

Erickson frequently makes the point that we are limited in our experience of new situations by excessive rigidity in the expectations we bring. Students of trance (and other state-altering experiences) quickly learn that the more familiar you are with an altered state of consciousness, the easier it is to achieve it. Thus Ericksonian scholars will quickly apprehend the richness of the teaching here. I suspect it will be underappreciated by those who don't have the cognitive set or take the time to experience its trance-inducing effects.

Jodie Wigren, MSW
Boston, Massachusetts

THE SILENT LANGUAGE OF PSYCHOTHERAPY, SECOND EDITION by Ernst G. Beier and David M. Young. *New York: Aldine, 1984, 292 pages, $29.95, hardcover.*

This book is a genuine pleasure to read and digest. It offers insights for therapists of any theoretical persuasion. It is especially useful for Ericksonian therapists, because of the emphasis on surprise and creativity in therapy. Beier and Young model the therapy process along interactional lines, while making their own contributions.

Beier's first edition, published in 1966, was a trailblazer in focusing on the importance of interactive issues in therapy. Rather than see influence in therapy as a one-way street, Beier suggested that the *patient* has as much impact on the therapist as the therapist on the patient, and went on to assert that it is this very impact that allows the therapist to be most helpful. Beier suggested the patient unconsciously strives to maintain his or her neurotic/psychotic compromise by eliciting certain responses from his social environment. When the patient enters the therapeutic hour, he or she will constrict the therapist's behavior so as to get reinforcement for that position. Beier argued the therapist must then provide a surprising response in an atmosphere of warmth which causes a sense of *beneficial uncertainty*. This uncertainty promotes an unconscious search for new behavior in the patient.

Beier and Young find that the basic ideas of the first volume have been supported by time. Today, the interactional view of psychotherapy is much more popular, and Beier and Young fall squarely in the middle of that view. Since 1966, there have been many research studies supporting the positions that Beier outlined. Beier and Young review many of these, but the well-read therapist will find other examples.

At the same time, Beier and Young agree with the analytic position that the origin of the suffering has to do with the adaptive compromise, the desire for two contradictory positions: I desire to be taken care of, and I also desire to be independent. To be depressed allows me to be taken care of while I can simultaneously deny that it is me doing it. After all, how could you not take care of such a depressed person?

Their position allows for a marriage of Freud and Skinner. The adaptive compromise suggests Freud, while the idea that the environment reinforces behavior and thus maintains it is a nod to the behaviorists.

Beier and Young suggest, for instance, that the patient who offends and upsets his therapist has found some gratification in the position that "nobody can stand me." While the origin of this position may be rooted in historical antecedents, the position is maintained by the social reinforcement value of the normal response to the patient's behavior.

The patient behaves in ways which make some responses likely and others difficult. When the therapist notices that his or her behaviors have been *constricted* by the patient, the intervention must be to behave in a surprising way, one which causes the sense of beneficial uncertainty. Beier and Young give many examples of classes of behavior which convey beneficial uncertainty to patients.

The concept of change of behavior in the therapist to change the behavior of the patient should be quite familiar to Ericksonian-oriented therapists. Beier puts great emphasis on the fact that when the patient unconsciously tries to manipulate the therapist, the most therapeutic response is to respond in an unexpected way. This surprise, done in an atmosphere of caring and concern, causes an unconscious search for new behaviors. Insight is not necessary;

the unconscious search is. Therapy with Beier, I have observed, could be conceptualized as a series of trances caused by the asocial, surprising responses.

Beier shies away from traditional hypnotic work in that he does not give directive therapeutic suggestions, believing that the search itself leads the patient to new, more adaptive behavior. In this paradigm, the answer is always inside the patient.

While this is an excellent work, I wondered about the inclusion of the chapter on play therapy with children. The chapter is too short to be any more than a series of hints, and lacks depth. The concept of play therapy seems quite curiously dated in this era of behaviorism and family therapy. Beier and Young discuss play therapy without presenting a clear rationale about when to do that and when to do family therapy. At the same time, readers of this monograph will remember that Erickson also liked to play with children therapeutically. This chapter, despite its flaws, should prove valuable for that reason.

One of Beier's most powerful contributions in my therapy supervision was the paradigmatic response. While there are some examples of that class of intervention given in the book, I believe there is not enough emphasis on it. I suppose that the therapist reading this book would be hard-pressed to create paradigmatic interventions, based only on the material in this volume. I wanted more here.

Similarly I hoped to see a discussion about Leary's interpersonal circle, especially the new revisions by Kiesler and Wiggins. This body of work, along with Benjamin's *Structural Analysis of Social Behavior*, has been a powerful tool of analysis in the area of interactional psychotherapy, and I am surprised that only passing reference is given to it here. Finally, there are occasional errors in copy editing. However, these are small problems, and all in all, the book is most delightful. I highly recommend it.

Lynn Johnson, Ph.D.
Salt Lake City, Utah